Pub Walks in Snowdonia

Laurence Main

Published by Sigma Leisure – an imprint of
Sigma Press, 1 South Oak Lane, Wilmslow, Cheshire SK9 6AR, England.

British Library Cataloguing in Publication Data
A CIP record for this book is available from the British Library.

ISBN: 1-85058-321-8

Typesetting and Design by: Sigma Press, Wilmslow, Cheshire.

Maps by: Morag Perrott

Text photographs: Laurence Main

Cover photograph: Ty Gwyn hotel, Roewen, on walk 1 (Laurence Main)

Printed by: Manchester Free Press

General Disclaimer

Whilst every effort has been made to ensure that the information given in this book is correct, neither the publisher nor the author accept any responsibility for any inaccuracy.

Preface

George Borrow, a great walker who also saw the insides of a few inns, reckoned that 'in the whole world there is no region more picturesquely beautiful than Snowdonia a region of mountains, lakes, cataracts and groves in which nature shows herself in her most grand and beautiful form'. Many would agree with him.

This mountain bastion is also an exotic land to the English. Welsh is still spoken here by most of the inhabitants, who retain their distinctive culture and rejoice in electing Plaid Cymru MPs. Perhaps that great key to the countryside, the Ordnance Survey map, is the most alien object. It is full of unpronounceable names. Walkers will keep seeing signposts pointing to 'Llwybr Cyhoeddus' (Welsh for 'public footpath').

The greatest tribute to the strength of local resistance was the investment by Edward I in the mighty castles which ring Snowdonia, such as Caernarfon, Conwy and Harlech. They are world heritage sites, yet it is the hills which attract the most attention.

They are only hills. Snowy hills, but rarely exceeding 3000 feet and with the highest peak measuring only 3560 feet above sea level. The vast majority of people can attain the summits and there's no need to acquire special equipment. These hills are accessible, but they give the impression of mountains. They are the highest in Britain south of the Scottish Highlands.

Some places are very popular. Snowdon can be like Picadilly Circus at times, while villages like Betws-y-Coed appear to exist for tourists. Snowdonia is surprisingly big, however. Pub walkers using this book cannot fail to reach parts other walkers never seem to reach. solitude is a quality of many beautiful, isolated spots, usually in the lesser-known southern half of the national park.

Getting around is not the problem it may appear to be in such a thinly-populated area. Planning is necessary but can also be great fun. Cars are not friendly to the environment. Use public transport to reach the starts of these walks. Rover tickets give excellent value for money. It is important, too, to contribute to the local economy by staying in the area and spending money here, rather than whizzing in from Manchester or wherever to yet another car park spoiling a Welsh valley and bringing food and drink with you. The locals are hospitable and can provide for you, as the pubs at the starts of these walks do. This is sheep country. Leave dogs at home.

Of course, if you aren't used to climbing 3000 feet, take things gradually by doing easier walks first. Allow plenty of time and be careful not to be caught out in the dark. As the best part of a climb is enjoying the view, choose good weather for your walks. Telephone 0839 505285 for a weather forecast. Expect sudden changes in the weather and take precautions.

Note landmarks when ascending so that you could find your way back down in the mist, if necessary, Always wear good walking boots. Carry spare clothing, including an anorak.

Ordnance Survey 1:25,000 scale Outdoor Leisure maps come into their own on these walks. Learn how to use them with a good compass. Practise with the routes in this book, then enjoy the freedom of making your own. There are enough hills, valleys and paths to last a lifetime, so come back frequently to take small areas in depth each time, rather than attempting to do too much in a short time superficially. Learn to love the land and it will share its secrets with you.

At the time of writing, Snowdonia National Park is entirely within the county of Gwynedd. English politicians propose breaking this up. Until they do, send an A5 SAE for free public transport map and timetables to the County Planning Officer, Gwynedd County Council, County Offices, Caernarfon, Gwynedd, LL55 1SH, tel. 0286 679535. Write for tourist information to the Snowdonia National Park Authority, National Park Office, Penrhyndeudraeth, Gwynedd, LL48 6LS, tel. 0766 770274 and to the Wales Tourist Board at 77 Conway Road, Colwyn Bay, Clwyd, LL29 7LN, tel. 0492 31731, for the northern half of Snowdonia, and to the

Wales Tourist Board at Canolfan Owain Glyndwr, Machynlleth, Powys, SY20 8EE, tel. 0654 702401, for the southern half.

Most of these walks were done on my own with the aid of Bws Gwynedd, the local bus network. James Webb, of the Meirionnydd Local Group of the Ramblers' Association, drove me to, and accompanied me on, some walks, as did the Rev. James McKnight and a National Park Warden, Richard Davies. A Dutch couple, Jolce and Harry Weerkamp, drove me to Snowdon and walked to the summit from Llanberis with me. When the clouds lifted at the top, revealing Crib Goch, they sportingly agreed to descend along it with me. They didn't know what was entailed until they were actually on the famous 'red ridge'. They coped very well and, I think, were glad of the experience. My wife, Paule, actually made it up Cadair Idris with me, while my three year-old daughter, Michelle, made light work of Aran Fawddwy.

Laurence Main

CONTENTS

Introduction

The Walks

Introduction

Snowdonia National Park was designated in 1951 and, with an area of 840 square miles, is the second largest in England and Wales (the Lake District is slightly larger). It is an ancient natural fortress of integrity and mystery.

At the top of the map are the Carneddau, the range of hills named after its two highest peaks, Carnedd Llewelyn (3485 feet) and Carnedd Dafydd (3424 feet). These are the names of the last native Prince of Wales and his brother. Llyn Geirionydd, above Trefriw, is just one of the lakes in this part. This is in the Conwy valley, marking the eastern boundary of Snowdonia. The hills rise steeply from it, forming a military barrier. Prehistoric remains abound in this region and old roads lead to a Neolithic axe factory at Graiglwyd, above the coastal resort of Penmaen-mawr. The fortified hilltop of Pen-y-Gaer stands on guard above Llan-bedr-y-cennin. The Romans built their strategic fortress nearby at Caer-hun. Walk east from Roewen along an old Roman road, past an even older megalithic tomb.

South of the A5 lie the Glyders, reaching 3279 feet with Glyder Fawr. Look down on Llyn Idwal from the ridge above the Devil's Kitchen (Twll Du – *the Black Hole*). All the features of glaciation are evident here, yet Darwin recalled spending many hours in Cwm Idwal in 1831 with Professor Adam Sedgwick, when 'neither of us saw a trace of the wonderful glacial phenomena all around us; we did not notice the plainly scored rocks, the perched boulders, the lateral and terminal moraines'. Snowdon itself stands grandly south of the Llanberis Pass. Pilgrims throng the paths to its summit, while more come up on the train. The easiest, safest and dullest route comes from Llanberis and stays near the railway. Take it to be sure of reaching your destination. When you have gained experience come back to explore the other paths. There's no pub at Pen y Pass now, but the youth hostel, bus stop and car park are convenient. Take the Pyg Track or the Miners' Path from here to the summit. These are both suitable for all the family. The adventurous can take the knife-edge reef of Crib Goch and return by way of a similar ridge on Y Lliwedd, the whole forming the Snowdon Horseshoe. Come from the south along the romantic Watkin Path, opened by the Prime Minister, Gladstone in 1892. On the western side there are the Rhyd Ddu and Snowdon Ranger paths.

The old port of Beddgelert (before Porthmadog's Cob was built, ships could reach it) is overlooked by Moel Hebog. The famous Cwm Pennant penetrates this range from the south-west. Of here it was said: 'O God, why didst Thou make Cwm Pennant so beautiful and the life of an old shepherd so short?'

Snowdonia used to be clothed by oak woodland and a remnant of this forms Coed Tremadog on the rocky escarpment overlooking the road between Tremadog and Beddgelert. Enter Snowdonia from Betws-y-Coed and encounter a number of beautiful passes and valleys. Moel Siabod stands above all of them, presenting a rugged front to the traveller from the south-east and reaching up to 2860 feet. The most spectacular hill is the 2265 feet of Cnicht, whose sharp features earned it the name of a knight because they resemble the shape of a knight's helmet. The round-headed Moelwyn Mawr (2527 feet) lies to its south.

Meirionnydd now beckons. There is a bonus of less intrusion by tourists to this southern half of the national park. The walking is the toughest in Wales if you care to explore the Rhinogs, however. With Y Llethr reaching 2475 feet, these hills are of a respectable height. Their chief feature is their starkness, in vivid contrast to the rich woodlands of the Vale of Ffestiniog around Maentwrog to their north. The Rhinogs display the oldest rocks to be found in Snowdonia, the Cambrian rocks that were laid down as sediments some 600 million years ago. Here are clefts and crags and tall heather. There are very few paths and the going is very hard. The Rhinogs are not for the inexperienced to get lost in. Yet old roads came this way, as the isolated Pont-Scethin shows. Prehistoric burial chambers, standing stones and stone circles abound.

The most unexplored part of Snowdonia is the large area east of the A470 as it approaches Blaenau Ffestiniog. The 2800 feet of Arenig Fawr rise out of the swamps and overlook Bala Lake (Llyn Tegid). The Roman fort of Tomen-y-Mur, now above the artificial reservoir of Llyn Trawsfynydd and its attendant nuclear power station, must have been one of the bleakest postings in the Empire. King Arthur was brought up with his foster-brother Sir Kay (Caius) at Caer Gai, near Llanuwchllyn.

This settlement could claim to be the Welshest of Welsh places. Its mountains are the Arans, with Aran Fawddwy's 2971 feet making it the highest peak in Britain south of the Snowdon range. It stands firm on traditional border territory. Mawddwy was included in Powys during the Middle Ages and its resident Red Bandits made it an independent enclave. The Afon Dyfi, the traditional border between north and south Wales, flows from the lake below Aran Fawddwy's summit.

Better known and more conspicuous is Cadair Idris – the Chair of Idris. At its feet stand the ruins of Castell y Bere, perhaps intended to become Llywelyn Fawr's capital of a Welsh state? Mary Jones set off from a nearby cottage to collect her famous Bible.

The Talyllyn Railway takes you down to the coast at Tywyn. The story of its preservation inspired many other such railways to cling or return to life. The scenic Cambrian Coast Line provides a link with the most southerly point of the National Park at Aberdyfi. The Romans used to cross the Dyfi nearby at Pennal, where they had a fort. The Tarrens are the last but not least of Snowdonia's peaks, with Tarren y Gesail being registered at 2187 feet. The slopes are thickly-wooded, unfortunately with quick-growing exotic conifers rather than with the natural climax vegetation of sessile oak.

'Whoever visits Wales sees her nakedness' commented a visitor around 1800. This was when the forest clearances of several centuries reached their climax. The remaining fragments of the primeval forest shelter badgers, polecats, grey squirrels (which have driven the red squirrels into the conifer plantations), wood mice, bank voles, hedgehogs, shrews, bats, dormice and a variety of birdlife, such as tits, woodpeckers, finches, thrushes, nuthatches, tree creepers, pied flycatchers, redstarts, wood warblers, jays and buzzards. The high corries of Snowdonia offer suitably damp conditions for mountain flowers even in hot summers. The Snowdon lily isn't found anywhere else in Europe nearer than the Alps. Holly fern, arctic and alpine mouse ear, alpine meadow-rue, hoary whitlow-grass, mountain avens, moss campion and alpine bistort also occupy the few lime-rich crags. Far more common is rough grassland, heather and peat bogs, reflecting the acid soils of the hills and moors. Eagles used to fly in the skies around Snowdonia's peaks but the birds of prey are now represented by buzzards and peregrines. Choughs like to nest in old mines and quarries. The little wrens can also provide the hillwalker with company and a song. Wheatears frequent the stony screes below the mountain cliffs. Skylarks and meadow pipits range over the grassy, rushy moorlands, while heather may shield red grouse. Even in summer, birdlife may be rare.

Mammals, apart from sheep, are even rarer. Feral goats are objects of excitement in the Rhinogs, as are deer in Coed y Brenin. Foxes may be seen, whereas stoats and polecats keep themselves to themselves. Field voles provide the buzzards with their food but conifer afforestation, by reducing the area of grassland, has deprived birds of prey of foraging areas. Similarly, the drainage of the peat-bogs has affected the snipe, lapwing, curlew and other birds. The pine marten may have survived because of the Forestry Commission plantations.

Members of the trout family include the gwyniad in Bala Lake (Llyn Tegid). It is found nowhere else in Wales and is a relic of the Ice Age. Sewin, or sea trout, come up the rivers, along with salmon. They lay their eggs in oxygenated waters far upstream. A few otters remain to feed on them. There is a unique inland colony of cormorants at Craig yr Aderyn (Bird Rock), near Tywyn.

The history of Wales is not well known in England. Many foreigners are surprised that the Welsh are a different people. The enduring symbol of this difference is the Welsh language. A visit to Snowdonia can only be enriched by learning a little of the language (if only enough to know how to pronounce the place names) and the history. This can extend into prehistoric time with the tales recorded in *The Mabinogion*.

The legend of the bells of Aberdyfi is one example of a story ostensibly set around 500 AD dating from about 3500 BC. There is evidence for some great flood then, suggesting that ancestral memory goes back further than the Celts and the Welsh language to the days of the standing stones and megalithic tombs. This was no remote fringe of Britain, Albion or whatever the island was called in those days. The evidence is that the people who erected the standing stones lived here in some numbers, especially overlooking the Cambrian Coast.

The Romans controlled the area by 78 AD. It would be wrong to conclude that they subdued it. The relationship was probably more like that with a client kingdom. The Irish settled in Snowdonia during the Roman Empire and immediately afterwards. They were pushed out by the mighty Cunedda (Kenneth) who came down with his eight sons from Manaw Gododdin, just north of Hadrian's Wall. He founded the strong dynasty in Gwynedd which lasted until the death of Llywelyn the Last in 1282. A great-grandson of Cunedda was the sixth century Maelgwn Gwynedd. a contemporary of King Arthur (whose kingdom was in South Wales, although he was overall war-lord for all of the British), Maelgwn was probably Sir Lancelot (a name based on the archaic French word for the stronger one who serves the weaker out of a sense of duty). King Arthur's last battle was at Camlan, near Dinas Mawddwy.

The Dark Ages were a golden age for the Celts and the Celtic form of Christianity prospered in the sixth century. The royal families supplied many of the saints. St Tydecho of Mawddwy, for instance, was a nephew of King Arthur (his mother was Ann of Gwent, a sister of Arthur). As the English gained control of most of Britain, they threatened to take Snowdonia too. The Welsh fiercely resisted them at times, relied upon Welsh weather to force invading armies home at others and tried to compromise at others. Even in Saxon times, the ruler of Gwynedd was prepared to accept the overlordship of the King of England in return for the English recognising that he did rule in Gwynedd. The semi-independent nature of this status was shown in 1157 when Owain Gwynedd paid homage to Henry II, but as a prince – the only Welsh lord to retain that title. Henry III officially recognised Llywelyn ap Gruffydd as Prince of Wales in 1267.

Pride comes before a fall and when Llywelyn tried to assert total independence by refusing to pay tribute or perform the act of homage to Henry III's successor, Edward I, he gave the English the excuse to conquer even Snowdonia. It did cost Edward I a lot in terms of very expensive castles. Harlech did become Owain Glyndwr's base for a while, but the sun of independence in Wales had set and patriots could only pray that the sea would swallow them up.

The Tudor accession to the throne of England could be seen as the red dragon finally overcoming the white and Celts once more ruling Saxons. Its effect was to accelerate the loss of native Welsh language and culture as ambitious Welshmen recognised their chance to succeed in England. Elizabeth I's reign did see the translation of the Bible into Welsh and the Welsh identity became involved with the Nonconformist movement. The passion for dissent also led to David Lloyd George, who was born at Llanystumdwy near Criccieth, just to the west of the national park, becoming a Liberal Prime Minister.

Lloyd George symbolised the talent that could come out of Wales, but the advent of universal education also brought official measures to discourage the speaking of Welsh. Education was in English only. Any child caught speaking Welsh was punished. At least the schools were full because there were thriving local communities based on the slate quarries and lead, copper and gold mines. As these closed, in the early 20th century, the native population declined. The English discovered a cheap haven to retire to or own second-homes in. The schools lost their pupils and closed. Later immigrants did bring children but they have to come very young if they are to learn Welsh. Luckily, the schools are now allowed to teach in Welsh and are one hope for the future of the language. Do your bit by trying to learn some Welsh pronunciations:

a	=	ah
c	=	k (hard)
ch	=	as in *loch*
dd	=	th in *the*
e	=	eh
f	=	v
ff	=	f
g	–	as in *go* (hard)
ngh	=	as in *anguish*
i	=	ee
ll	=	say *l*, keep tongue in this position and gently blow
o	=	oh
th	=	as in *through* (not as in *the*)
w	=	often as *oo*, with cwm (valley) sounding as coomb
y	=	as e in *the* (y or yr), or as *i*, so that Dyffryn sounds like *derffrin*

There are mutations in Welsh, making *Llanberis* the sacred enclosure (*llan*) of *Peris* (p mutates to b). Similarly *Llanbedr* refers to St Peter (*Pedr*).

Some common place names use the following words:

aber	=	estuary, river-mouth or confluence
afon	=	river
bach, fach	=	small
bedd	=	grave
betws	=	chapel or oratory
blaen	=	head of the valley
bont, pont	=	bridge
braich	=	arm
brith	=	speckled
bryn	=	hill
bwlch	=	pass, defile
bychan	=	little
cadair	=	chair
cae	=	field
caer	=	fort
capel	=	chapel
carn, carnedd	=	pile of stones
carreg	=	rock
castell	=	castle
cau	=	deep hollow
cefn	=	ridge
celli, gelli	=	grove
ceunant	=	ravine
clogwyn	=	precipice
coch	=	red
coed	=	woodland
congl	=	corner
cors, gors	=	bog
craig	=	rock
crib	=	narrow ridge
croes	=	cross
cwm	=	cirque, valley
dinas	=	fort
dol, ddol	=	meadow
drws	=	door
dwr	=	water

dwy	=	two
dyffryn	=	valley
eglwys	=	church
eira	=	snow
esgair	=	mountain shoulder
fawr, mawr	=	big
felin, melin	=	mill
ffordd	=	road
ffridd	=	mountain pasture
ffynnon	=	well, spring
foel, moel	=	rounded hill
fynydd, mynydd	=	mountain
gam	=	crooked
glan	=	bank, shore
glas, las	=	blue, green
glyder	=	heap
glyn	=	glen
gwastad	=	plain, level ground
gwern	=	marsh
gwyn	=	white
gwynt	=	wind
hafod, hafotty	=	summer dwelling
hen	=	old
hendre	=	winter dwelling
hir	=	long
isa, isaf	=	lower
llan	=	sacred enclosure, church
llechwedd	=	hillside
llethr	=	slope
llwyd	=	grey
llwyn	=	grove
llyn	=	lake
maen	=	stone
maes	=	field
morfa	=	coastal marsh
mur	=	wall
nant	=	brook, stream
newydd	=	new
oer	=	cold
ogof	=	cave

oleu	=	light
pant	=	small hollow
pen	=	head, top
penrhyn	=	promontory
pentre, pentref	=	village
pistyll	=	spout, cataract
plas	=	mansion
pwll	=	pool
rhaeadr	=	waterfall
rhiw	=	hill
rhos	=	moorland, marsh
rhyd	=	ford
ucha, uchaf	=	upper
uwch	=	above
waun	=	moor
y	=	the, of the
yn	=	in
ynys	=	island
ysgol	=	school, ladder
ysgubor	=	barn
ystrad	=	valley floor, strath
sarn	=	paved way, causeway
sych	=	dry
tal	=	end
tan	=	under
tarren	=	hill
tir	=	land
tomen	=	mound
traeth	=	stretch of shore
tre	=	town, hamlet
tri	=	three
trwyn	=	nose, promontory
twll	=	hole
ty	=	house
tyddyn	=	smallholding

If you can say nothing else, do try this:

Good morning	=	Bore da *(bor-eh-da)*
Thank you	=	diolch *(dee-olc)*

Real Ale

Wales is the home of real water, which can be drunk straight from the tap. Some, such as Cerist mineral water from near Dinas Mawddwy, is bottled and sold in England. St David was known as the water-drinker. Even so, the Welsh do drink beer. Nonconformist conscience may have persuaded many to stick to tea, but this is an indefensible practice. Tea has nothing to do with Wales, while the tea plantations in countries like Sri Lanka exploit cheap local labour and deprived them of land to grow valuable food on. The cash for the tea crop doesn't reach them. Ale is a much more traditional drink. Indeed, Wales has the Celtic link with whisky. Nowadays it is Brecon that has a distillery but Bala used to have one. Ale was traditionally drunk because it was safer than water. Perhaps Welsh ale isn't as good as English because Welsh water was that much better. Where we do have a pub brewing its own beer, the quality of the local water is claimed to enhance it. Ale in the Middle Ages was thick, sticky and sweet. Hops weren't introduced until the 15th century, adding preservative qualities as well as bitterness and flavour. Sugar was later added to the list of ingredients (water, barley, hops yeast and sugar).

Each of the pubs featured in this book serves real ale on draught. This means that the beers are still fermenting when they leave the brewery. This is known as secondary fermentation because it supplements the primary fermentation which took place in the brewery's large brewing vessels. The process continues at a slow pace as the barrels are racked in the pub cellar. Carbon dioxide is produced and escapes through a spile hole. The thirsty walker may received gravity drawn beer, direct from the barrel, or beer from a hand pump or electric pump attached to the bar. Apart from this pumping, real ale is free of the carbon dioxide or nitrogen oxide used to force pasteurised (ie where the fermentation has been killed off) varieties under pressure out of their kegs. These gassy beers are the ones that need the glossy adverts. They are shunned by lovers of traditional ales. Many landlords take a different view, however.

Traditional real ale is less easy to keep. Great care has to be taken regarding temperature and cleanliness. The draught beer has a very short 'shelf-life' and it takes skill, acquired from both training and experience, to serve a good pint of real ale.

Opening Hours

Under recent legislation pubs in England and Wales can now open for a maximum of 12 hours each day on Mondays to Saturdays (being 11am to 11pm) and for six and a half hours on Sundays (being noon to 3pm and 7pm to 10.30pm) unless extensions have been granted by local licensing magistrates. In Wales, however, there is a tradition of pubs being closed all day on Sundays. This practice still applies in the district of Dwyfor, including Tremadog and Beddgelert. Most country pubs do not find it in their interest to take full advantage of the 'relaxed' hours during the week and tend to stick to the 'traditional' hours of noon to 3pm and 6pm to 11pm or 7pm to 11pm. Check each pub individually.

The Walks

Each walk in this book follows rights of way to which you, as a member of the public, have unrestricted access, or agreed courtesy paths where dogs are not allowed. Should you come across any problems, send full details (including grid references) to the Director of Highways, Gwynedd County Council, County Offices, Caernarfon, Gwynedd, LL55 1SH, tel. 0286 679536. Do send a copy of your letter to the Ramblers' Association. If it concerns the northern part of the national park, write to Frank Skelcey, 12 Gwydyr Road, Dolgarrog, Conwy, Gwynedd, LL32 8JS. If it is in Meirionnydd, covering the southern part of the national park, write to your author, Laurence Main, 9 Mawddwy Cottages, Minllyn, Dinas Mawddwy, Machynlleth, SY20 9LW.

Public footpath, in Welsh

The walks are numbered in sequence from north to south and are spread all over Snowdonia, with a slight bias to Meirionnydd, which has been neglected by other authors. Use the Ordnance Survey Outdoor Leisure maps as detailed for each walk. They are marvellous keys to the countryside and only three maps are needed to cover all of the national park. The walks average seven miles in length and some can be linked together to form longer routes, if desired, being:

Walks 1 (Roewen) and 2 (Llanbedr-y-cennin) connect to make an 11 mile route

Walks 5 (Swallow Falls) and 6 (Betws-y-Coed) combine to form a 9 mile route

Walks 10 (Gellilydan) and 11 (Trawsfynydd) together give a ramble of $11^1/_2$ miles

Walks 12 (Bala Lake/Llyn Tegid) and 14 (Llanuwchllyn) can be joined by a short ride on the Bala Lake Railway to allow a day's walk of some 12 miles

Walks 18 (Penmaenpool) and 19 (Dolgellau) can be linked by a short bus ride (no 28) or a hike along the dismantled railway line to give a day's walk of at least 13 miles

Walks 20 (Aran Fawddwy) and 25 (Mallwyd) could be joined together at Dinas Mawddwy to give a very long day's walk of 23 miles

Walks 22 (Mary Jones' Cottage) and 23 (Tal-y-llyn) can be connected to form a ramble of $15^1/_2$ miles.

All walks should be within the capabilities of anyone of average fitness. Allow about one hour for every two miles, except for the higher climbs, such as Cadair Idris, Aran Fawddwy and Snowdon, where it may take you one hour to climb one mile. It's always sensible to allow extra time for the mountains to avoid being caught out at dusk. Keep to the path and treat it as a privilege to walk across someone else's land; in that way we can build an atmosphere of co-operation, rather than confrontation, in the countryside.

The Country Code

❏ Guard against all risk of fire

❏ Fasten all gates (NB this is the official advice. In practice, sheep farmers usually leave gates open on purpose so that sheep can reach water etc, so 'leave gates as you find them')

❏ Keep dogs under proper control

❏ Avoid damaging fences, hedges and walls

❏ Keep to paths across farmland

❏ Leave no litter

❏ Safeguard water supplies

❏ Protect wildlife, wild plants and trees

❏ Go carefully on country roads

❏ Respect the life of the countryside

Take the bus to the starts of these walks!

1. ROEWEN

Route: Ty Gwyn Hotel, Roewen – Rhiw youth hostel – Cae Coch – Llangelynin Old Church – Ty Gwyn Hotel, Roewen

Distance: 6 miles

Map: O.S. Outdoor Leisure 17 (Snowdonia-Snowdon & Conwy Valley areas)

Start: Ty Gwyn Hotel, Roewen (SH 759719)

Ty Gwyn, Roewn

Access: Roewen is on a minor road one mile west of the B5106 at Ty'n-y-groes, about four miles south of Conwy. Bus no 19 (running between Llandudno and Llanberis) stops at the crossroads on the eastern side of Roewen. Cars may be parked near the Ty Gwyn Hotel.

Ty Gwyn Hotel, Roewen (0492 650232)

This picturesque pub retains its hotel title without offering accommodation anymore. The real ale is good, however (being J.W. Lees Bitter from an independent brewery in

Manchester). Food is available, while there is a riverside beer garden. Drovers called here in the 16th century. Opening hours are 11am to 11pm on weekdays, noon to 3pm and 7pm to 10.30pm on Sundays.

Llangelynin Old Church

At 927 feet above sea level, this is one of the highest churches in Wales. St Celynin founded it in the seventh century and his holy well, Ffynnon Gelynin, is in a corner of the graveyard. Everything is ancient around here, from the drovers' road through the old forest of Parc Mawr to the standing stones and burial chamber beside the relatively recent Roman road which passes Rhiw youth hostel. The views are inspiring, so don't forget to put a film in your camera!

The Walk

1. Go right along the village street and bear right when the road forks.

2. Fork left along the old Roman road to pass Rhiw youth hostel, standing stones and a prehistoric burial chamber.

3. Turn right at Cae Coch to follow a waymarked track along the slopes of Tal-y-fan. Pass Caer Bach (a mound) on your left, then the conical hill of Craig Celynin on your right. Continue along the left side of a wall and descend to Llangelynin Old Church.

4. Go down the old drovers' road which plunges steeply down through the forest of Parc Mawr.

5. Bear slightly left down a lane. Reach a T junction and turn right to walk back down to Roewen.

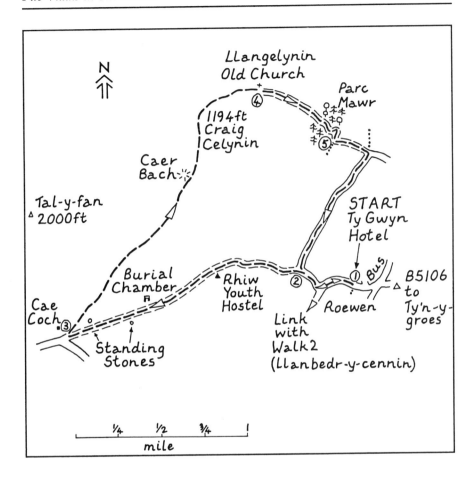

Llangelynin
Old Church

Parc
Mawr

1194ft
Craig
Celynin

Caer
Bach

Tal-y-fan
△ 2000ft

START
Ty Gwyn
Hotel

Burial
Chamber

Rhiw
Youth
Hostel

Cae
Coch

Standing
Stones

Roewen

Link
with
Walk 2
(Llanbedr-y-cennin)

B5106
to
Ty'n-y-
groes

¼   ½   ¾   1
mile

N

2. LLANBEDR-Y-CENNIN

Route: Ye Olde Bull Inn, Llanbedr-y-cennin – Llwyn-y-gwaew – Roewen – Pontwgan – Ye Olde Bull Inn, Llanbedr-y-cennin

Distance: 5 miles

Map: O.S. Outdoor Leisure 17 (Snowdonia-Snowdon & Conwy Valley areas)

Start: Ye Olde Bull Inn, Llanbedr-y-cennin (SH 761695)

Access: Llanbedr-y-cennin is at the junction of minor roads about one mile to the west of the B5106 road at Caerhun, five miles south of Conwy. If you come by bus (no 19 running between Llandudno and Llanberis), alight at Roewen, where this route can be linked with Walk 1 to form an 11 mile route.

Ye Olde Bull Inn, Llanbedr-y-cennin (0492 660508)

Drovers used this old inn which has a good reputation for meals (book in advance to be sure of a place). Bar snacks and real ales are always available. Opening hours are 7pm to 11pm on Mondays, noon to 3pm and 7pm to 11pm from Tuesdays to Fridays, 11.30am to 3pm and 7pm to 11pm on Saturdays, noon to 3pm and 7pm to 10.30pm on Sundays. Pilgrims also came here on visits to a nearby holy well, Ffynnon Bedr (now on private land).

Caerhun

The Roman fort of *Canovium* was on the coast road between Chester and Caernarfon. The principal road to South Wales, known as Sarn Helen, started from here. This was a very important strategic spot, with a British hill fort occupying the summit of nearby Pen-y-Gaer. Caerhun is now the most reliable place in Snowdonia to find hawfinch. Woodpeckers, goldfinch, greenfinch, redpoll, jay, jackdaw and buzzard may also be seen. The fields on these damp hillsides are dotted with both sheep and cattle. Welsh Blacks are kept for both dairy and beef production.

The Walk

1. Bear left on the uphill road and go right at a fork with a No Through Road to keep climbing. Pen-y-Gaer looms above on your left. Pass a second No Through Road on your left. Go ahead around a bend in the road on your right.

2. Turn right through a gate to take a signposted public footpath. Follow its firm track through the farmyard at Llwyn-y-gwaew and continue along a grass track with a fence on your right to reach a lane. Go left uphill with the lane. Pass under power lines supported by a giant pylon on your left. Reach a public footpath signpost on your right.

3. Turn right along the signposted path, taking the aged wooden ladder stile beside a gate and aiming for a gap in the far right-hand corner ahead. Continue beside a wall surmounted by a fence on your right and take another aged wooden ladder stile in the wall ahead, just to the left of the corner. Go ahead and bear right above an old sunken lane. Cross a wall ahead by another ancient ladder stile (50 yards to the left of a gate).

4. Walk above the sunken lane on your right. Turn left over iron steps in the next corner. Turn right immediately to continue above the sunken lane. Go through the bottom gate and bear right with a track down to a farm. Pass the farmhouse on your right and turn left to cross the bridge over the Afon Roe. Go right down a lane into Roewen.

5. Pass the Ty Gwyn Hotel on your left (where this route can be linked with one starting from Roewen). Turn right along a signposted public footpath, passing Huw Edwards' Memorial Stone on your left. Cross a footbridge over the Afon Roe. Go ahead between walls and past meadows on your left. Turn left before Glasgoed farmhouse to reach the river. Go right to walk with the river on your left until a road bridge crosses it.

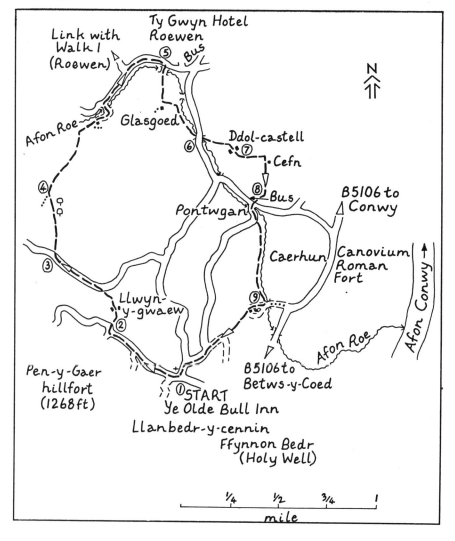

GWLADGARWR • UNDEBWR LLAFUR • SOSIALYDD • LLENOR
OR GRAIG HON Y'M NADDWYD
1892
HUW T. EDWARDS
1970
WELSH PATRIOT • HEWN FROM THE ROCK • AUTHOR
• TRADE UNIONIST • SOCIALIST •

MAN GENI / PLACE OF BIRTH
PEN-FFRIDD, RO-WEN.

MYNYDD YR OERWYNT MINIOG - A DIDDOS
HEN DYDDYN Y FAWNOG,
LLE'R OEDD SGLEIN AR BOB CEINIOG
A 'NHAID O'R LLAID YN DWYN LLOG.
H.T.E.

6. Go left through a kissing-gate to turn left across the bridge, then turn right to cross the road and follow a signposted public footpath down steps. Cross a field to take a gate to the left of a farmhouse ahead. Pass through the farmyard, cross a stream and reach an opening to the first field on your left.

7. Turn left up the field to walk beside a wall on your right and under power lines. Cross a stile on your right in the top corner and turn left up the next field towards a house. Go right to follow its iron fence on your left. Bear left over a stile in the corner and turn right immediately over metal steps. Go ahead along the crest of this field to take more steps and continue beside a hedge on your left.

8. Go through the right-hand of two gaps in the hedge ahead. Descend with a hedge on your left and bear left through a gate just to the right of a barn. Go down to a road at a junction where there is a bus stop. Take the road over the bridge ahead and turn left down a signposted public footpath which uses a metal ladder to cross the hedge. Descend to the river and go right to walk with it on your left until a bridge crosses it.

9. Turn right along a concrete lane going away from the bridge. Fork right to pass a farm on your left and take a gate just to the right of the farmhouse. Bear very slightly right to a waymarked gate and go ahead with a hedge on your right in the next field. Cross a ladder stile in the corner to go ahead along a firm track, then maintain your direction when it joins a road back to Llanbedr-y-cennin and Ye Olde Bull Inn.

3. TREFRIW

Route: The Fairy Falls Inn, Trefriw – Llyn Geirionydd – The Fairy Falls Inn, Trefriw

Distance: 6 miles

Map: O.S. Outdoor Leisure 17 (Snowdonia-Snowdon & Conwy Valley areas)

Start: The Fairy Falls Inn, Trefriw (SH 782632)

Access: The Fairy Falls Inn is beside the B5106 in Trefriw, just over the bridge and on the opposite side from the woollen mill. There are bus stops (for nos 19, 49 and 65 from Llanrwst, where there is a railway station, nos 19 and 48 also come from Llandudno) and a car park nearby.

The Fairy Falls Inn, Trefriw (0492 640250)

Crown Prince Hussein of Jordan ate a steak pie with chips here in 1989. He missed the Welsh singing on Friday nights. As a devout Moslem (born of a British mother) he wouldn't have sampled the real ale, either. Bed and breakfast is also available at this colourful place. Opening hours are noon to 11pm on weekdays, noon to 3pm and 7pm to 10.30pm on Sundays.

Trefriw

Hydro-electricity from the Afon Crafnant powers the woollen mill at
Trefriw. Visit it between 9am and 5.30pm from Monday to Friday to see
all the processes in the manufacture of tapestries and tweeds. The shop
is also open at weekends. Llyn Geirionydd's clear water betrays the fact
that it is so polluted by lead that plants and fish cannot survive in it. It is
used for canoeing, sailing and water skiing. The monument is to Taliesin, the Chief of Bards, who lived near here for a while in the sixth
century.

The Walk

1. Go left to cross the bridge over the Afon Crafnant and pass the
   woollen mill on your right. Turn right up a steep lane which bears
   left. Go left at a junction and almost immediately take a path on your
   right. Reach a road and go right down it to pass a house on your left.

2. Turn left up a woodland path.

3. Ignore a path coming from your left. Bear slightly right to continue
   past a wall on your left. Descend to the lake and go right to reach the
   monument to Taliesin.

4. Follow the lakeside path, with forest on your right and the lake on
   your left. Bear slightly away from the lake at its far end, then turn left
   along a track.

5. Go left along the lane to pass the lake on your left, continue over a
   stile and fork left along a narrow path through bracken.

6. Follow the track ahead, above the stream on your left.

7. Cross the bridge over the Afon Crafnant and turn right with a road
   back down to Trefriw and the Fairy Falls Inn.

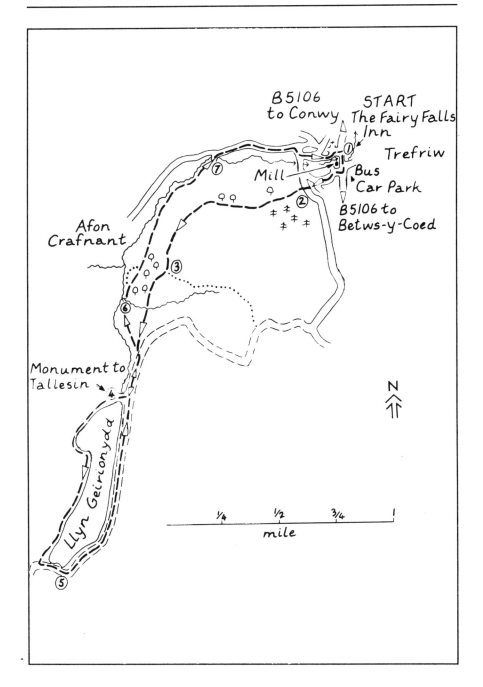

4. SNOWDON

Route: Prince of Wales Hotel, Llanberis – Llanberis Path – Snowdon – Llanberis Path – Prince of Wales Hotel, Llanberis

Distance: 10 miles

Map: O.S. Outdoor Leisure 17 (Snowdonia-Snowdon & Conwy Valley areas)

Start: Prince of Wales Hotel, Llanberis (SH 578603)

Access: The Prince of Wales Hotel is in the High Street, Llanberis, which is on the A4086 nine miles east of Caernarfon. Buses run to Llanberis from Caernarfon (Nos 11 and 88), Bangor (No 77) and Llandudno (No 19).

Prince of Wales Hotel, Llanberis (0286 870708)

Accommodation is available in this old inn, as is real ale and food. Opening hours are 11am to 11pm on weekdays, noon to 3pm and 7pm to 10.30pm on Sundays.

Snowdon

Even pub walkers must climb Snowdon, the highest mountain in Wales. The Llanberis Path is the easiest and the most popular of the routes to its 3560 feet summit. Even so, it can be dangerous in bad weather or in winter. In particular, don't be caught out at dusk! Allow at least six hours to complete this route. The proximity of the railway may tempt you into taking out a second mortgage in order to buy a ticket for the train ride down. Alternatively, there's nothing better than Crib Goch's pencil thin ridge on a fine day (then take a bus back from Pen-y-pass to Llanberis). You'll need good footwear for this exciting route. The Snowdon Mountain Railway is the only rack railway in Britain and will take you back to the eastern end of Llanberis, from where you turn left and fork left into the High Street. Telephone 0286 870223 for details of the

Snowdon Mountain Railway's services. Llanberis also has its Lake Railway (tel. 0286 870549). Visit the Power of Wales exhibition in Llanberis (tel. 0286 870636).

Two happy tourists at the summit of Snowdon

The Walk

1. Go left along Llanberis' High Street. Pass Padarn Lake Hotel on your left. Pass St Padarn's Church on your right, then turn right along Church Lane (signposted for Ceunant Mawr Waterfalls). Follow the lane under a bridge carrying the Snowdon Mountain Railway.

2. Turn right at a T junction to pass Maes Derlwyn on your right. Climb with the lane over a cattle grid beside which is a kissing-gate and a No Through Road sign. Pass a plantation of conifer trees on your left. Pass a seasonal cafe on your left, take a gate across the lane and pass the final car park on your left.

3. Turn left off the lane at a notice board which shows the Llanberis Path and surrounding access land. Take the gate to follow the signposted track to the summit of Snowdon. This broad track is obvious, and may be crowded with walkers. It gives a view of the Snowdon Mountain Railway on your right.

4. Follow the path through a tunnel under the railway, so that any passing trains will now be on your left. Pass the halfway House (1750 feet above sea level), look down on Llyn Du'r Arddu and climb to renew acquaintance with the railway.

5. Pass under the railway again and turn right to climb to the summit. Do not be tempted to follow the railway. Climb above the summit station and cafe to admire the view from the summit.

6. Retrace your steps from the 3560 feet summit of Snowdon down to Llanberis and the Prince of Wales Hotel.

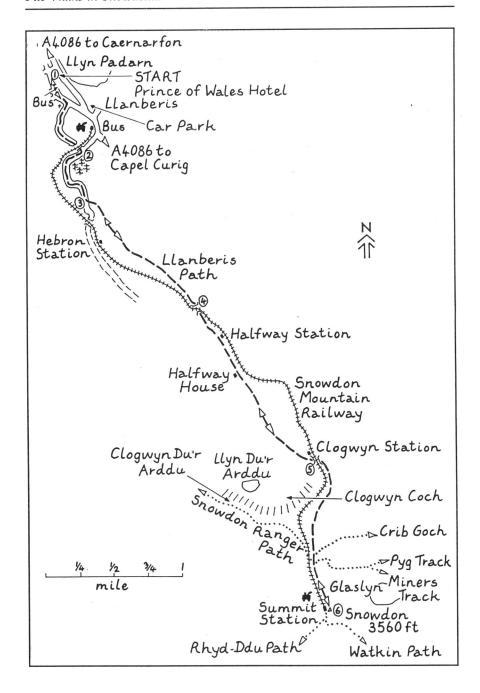

5. SWALLOW FALLS

Route: Swallow Falls Hotel – Ugly House – Swallow Falls – Miners'
Bridge – Artists' Wood Walk – Swallow Falls Hotel

Distance: 4 miles

Map: O.S. Outdoor Leisure 17 (Snowdonia: Snowdon & Conwy Valley
areas)

Start: Swallow Falls Hotel (SH 765577)

Access: The Swallow Falls Hotel is beside the A5 about two miles west
of Betws-y-Coed. There is a large car park here, while buses Nos 19
(Llandudno – Llanberis) and 95 (Llanrwst – Bangor) stop here.

The Swallow Falls Hotel (0690 710796)

The rooms were decorated with valuable murals by Norman Webster in
1949. Stay here on a bed and breakfast basis. The RAF used it as a
convalescent home during the Second World War. Now there is a busy
gift shop and a Welsh fudge pantry. Real ale and food are available.
Opening hours are 11am to 11pm on weekdays, noon to 3pm and 7pm
to 10.30pm on Sundays.

The Swallow Falls

You could pay to see these when you cross the road directly from the
hotel. This walk gives you a free view. The name comes from the Welsh
word 'ewynnol' (foaming). George Borrow recorded in his *Wild Wales*
(1862) how 'The Fall of the Swallow is not a majestic single fall, but a
succession of small ones'. He rewarded his local woman guide with
sixpence (a generous sum in 1854). The pool 'black as death and
seemingly of great depth' is said to contain the spirit of Sir John Gwynne
of Gwydir, in the hope that the water will purify its evil. The Ugly
House (Ty-hyll) was built quickly without mortar to conform with the
law that any free man could have the rights over the land his new house
stood on if he could raise a roof and have smoke coming from its
chimney within one day. Look out for grey wagtails near the river.

A waterfall on the Afon Llugwy, seen from east of Swallow Falls

The Walk

1. Cross the A5 road carefully and turn left along its pavement. Turn right over a bridge opposite the Ugly House (Ty-hyll).

2. Turn right along the signposted public footpath, going down steps to follow a riverside path across meadows. Enter woodland and soon pass above the superb Swallow Falls, on your right. Shortly afterwards fork left to climb away from the river but soon return to run high above it. Bear left up a track and immediately after a house go half right down a path. Cross a footbridge and bear left to climb steps on your right up to a road.

3. Go right along the road through the forest, above the river on your right. After nearly a mile, when the road bears left, turn right down through the woodland to reach the Miners' Bridge.

4. YOU COULD LINK THIS ROUTE WITH THAT FROM BETWS-Y-COED HERE TO GIVE A CIRCUIT OF NINE MILES.
   To complete this walk, however, do cross the bridge and turn right along the signposted Artists' Wood Walk. This delightful path keeps near the Afon Llwgwy on your right until a ruin marks where you bear left to reach the A5 road. Go right along its pavement to return to the Swallow Falls Hotel, on your left.

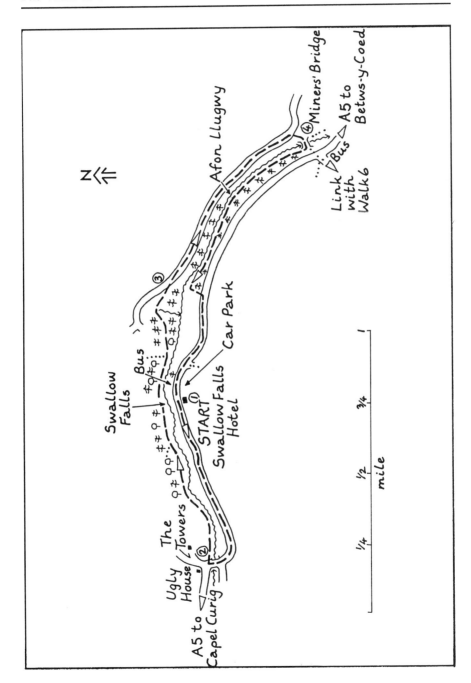

6. BETWS-Y-COED

Route: Royal Oak Hotel, Betws-y-Coed – Llyn Elsi – Sarn Helen – Miners' Bridge – Royal Oak Hotel, Betws-y-Coed

Distance: 5 miles

Map: O.S. Outdoor Leisure 17 (Snowdonia-Snowdon & Conwy Valley areas)

Start: Royal Oak Hotel, Betws-y-Coed (SH 793565)

Access: Betws-y-Coed is near the junction of the A5 with the A470. It has a railway station for trains from Llandudno and Blaenau Ffestiniog. Bus no 19 comes from Llanberis and Llandudno; bus no 67 runs here between Bala and Llandudno, while bus no 95 passes through between Bangor and Llanrwst.

The Royal Oak Hotel, Betws-y-Coed (0690 710219)

The Stables Bar is open from 11am to 11pm on weekdays, noon to 3pm and 7pm to 10.30pm on Sundays. Real ale and food are available, as is bed and breakfast. Dating from the first half of the 19th century, this hotel is where the artists J.M.W. Turner and David Cox stayed when painting in the area.

Betws-y-Coed

Pronounced *Bet-oos* and not *Betsy*, this is a sacred spot in the woods. Artists, including the Birmingham water-colourist David Cox, recognised it as such. It is also a route centre and houses the delightful Conwy Valley Railway Museum. Sarn Helen passed nearby. Miners' Bridge stands close to where this Roman road crossed the Afon Llugwy. Miners used to take the bridge between their homes and the lead mines on the plateau to the north of the village.

The Walk

1. Go left through Betws-y-Coed, passing the Climber and Rambler shop on your left. Pass Betws-y-Coed Pottery on your left, then turn left up steps in the wall next to a bus stop, which has a public footpath sign affixed to it. Follow a narrow zigzag path up through woodland to a broad, grassy track.

2. Go left a few paces and turn sharply right uphill to follow the narrow woodland path that is waymarked by green paint on rocks. Climb to a wide track and bear left along it to a clearing where it continues as a narrow woodland path waymarked by green paint on rocks. This sinuous path climbs to another firm track near a white-topped post.

3. Go ahead across the track and up the narrow forest path, still waymarked by green paint on rocks. Follow it through a gap in a wall and eventually reach a wide, grassy track. Turn left along it.

4. When a firm track converges with yours from the left, turn left across the firm track and take a waymarked woodland path which leads to a view point over Llyn Elsi. Descend to a monument recording the fact that the Earl of Ancaster gave this lake to the local waterworks on 18th June 1914.

5. Turn sharply right (as directed by a blue waymark) to take another path back to the firm track. Cross it to follow a path near the edge of the forest, soon walking with a wall on your right. Go ahead over a ladder stile and walk with the forest's perimeter fence on your left to the buildings of Hafod-las.

6. Turn left just before the buildings and cross a ladder stile beside a gate to climb with a track to a junction. Turn right along a firm forest track. Turn right at a T junction, ignore the first track on your left but take the second to go through the gate for Pant yr Hyddod. Pass this house on your right, continue through a gate, up a slope and eventually descend towards the corner of a forest on your left.

7. Turn right along a track, away from the forest and with a wall on your left. This is the old Roman road Sarn Helen. Cross a firm track to continue through gates waymarked with blue paint. Cross another

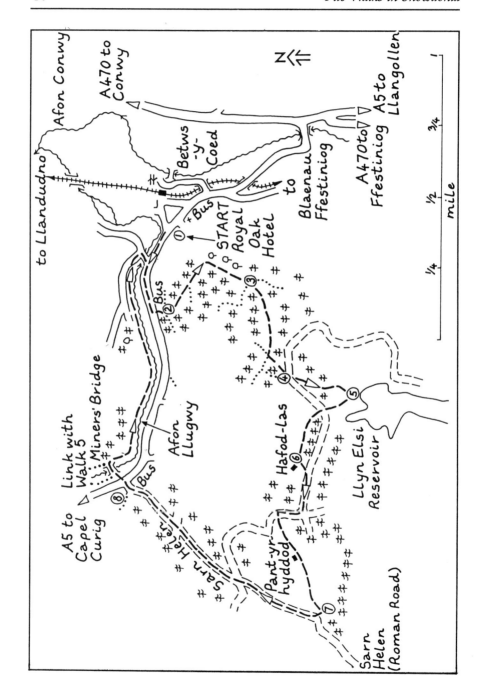

track and a footbridge as you descend. Go ahead over a ladder stile beside a gate and reach the A5 road near a bus stop.

8. Cross the road to take the signposted public footpath through the forest ahead. Approach a footbridge (Miners' Bridge).
IF YOU WISH TO LINK THIS WALK WITH THAT FROM THE SWALLOW FALLS HOTEL, DO NOT GO DOWN THE STEPS TO THE BRIDGE. Do turn left along the Artist's Wood Walk.
TO CONTINUE THIS ROUTE, CROSS THE MINERS' BRIDGE OVER THE AFON LLYGWY. Turn right to follow the path above the river on your right. Turn right over a bridge, Pont-y-Pair. Turn left to retrace your steps back through Betws-y-Coed to the Royal Oak Hotel, which is on your right.

The Stables Bar, Royal Oak Hotel

7. BEDDGELERT

Route: Royal Goat Hotel, Beddgelert – Cwm-cloch – Moel Hebog – Royal Goat Hotel, Beddgelert

Distance: 5 miles

Map: O.S. Outdoor Leisure 17 (Snowdonia-Snowdon & Conwy Valley areas)

Start: Royal Goat Hotel, Beddgelert (SH 588480)

Access: The Royal Goat Hotel is on the western edge of Beddgelert, beside the A498. Buses nos 11 (Llanberis – Caernarfon) and 97 (from Porthmadog) stop nearby.

The Royal Goat Hotel, Beddgelert (0766 86224)

The new Japanese emperor stayed here when he was the crown prince. The oriental connection is in the tradition of Ingrid Bergman and the cast of the film *Inn of the Sixth Happiness*. Another film star to stay here was Joan Whaley (star of the film *Willow*). Prince Arthur of Connaught also spent the night here. Bed and breakfast is available to you, as are food and real ale. The first landlord, in 1801, was David Pritchard, who invented the 'grave of Gelert' near the village. His old retainer now haunts the hotel. As Beddgelert is in Dwyfror, it must be 'dry' on Sundays, but the bar is open from 11am to 11pm on weekdays.

Moel Hebog

Moel Hebog is Beddgelert's mountain. It looks much more than 2566 feet high, although its top is quite flat ('moel' means bald or rounded hill). 'Hebog' means falcon or hawk. Apart from marking the boundaries of farms, the walls on it also divide the 'ffridd' (lower pasture, where sheep spend the winter) from the 'mynydd' (high, summer pasture). You may see a peregrine falcon from this mountain, which would thus justify its name. Sygun Copper Mine, Beddgelert is open to visitors (tel. 0766 86595).

The Walk

1. Go left and immediately left up the drive to pass the Royal Goat Hotel on your left. Turn right with a signposted path through a gate. Continue through another gate and with a wall on your right. Bear left with a track and continue up the drive to Cwm-cloch farm.

2. Turn right to cross a stile and continue through a gap in a wall to a second stile. Bear left with the cairned path, which bears right to cross another wall. Follow a grassy path to the ridge, where the cairned path goes uphill on your left.

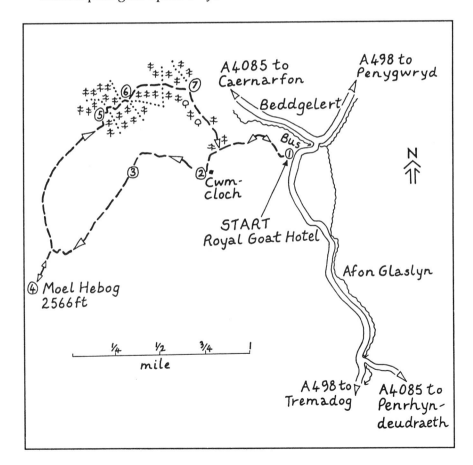

3. Take a gate in the wall ahead and follow a path which climbs to a large cairn before going left to the 2566 feet high summit of Moel Hebog.

4. Return to the large cairn and continue down the ridge. Descend to the edge of a forest and go left down to a corner.

5. Turn right over a low fence, bear left to cross a wall and go right a few paces down a forest track. Follow a walled path down to another forest track.

6. Go right for 50 yards along the track, then turn left to follow a path running beside a wall on your left. When the field on your left ends, bear right and cross a forest track.

7. Turn right along the next track to follow it back to your outward route. Go left to retrace your steps to Beddgelert's Royal Goat Hotel.

The Royal Goat, Beddgelert

8. TREMADOG

Route: The Golden Fleece Inn, Tremadog – Lawrence of Arabia's birth-place – Cwm Mawr – Cae-glan-yr-afon – Fach-goch – The Golden Fleece Inn, Tremadog

Distance: 6 miles

Map: O.S. Outdoor Leisure 18 (Snowdonia – Harlech & Bala areas)

Start: The Golden Fleece Inn, Tremadog (SI I 561401)

Access: The Golden Fleece Inn is in the Market Square (Sgwar y Farchnad) in the centre of Tremadog, at the junction of the A487 and A498 roads one mile north of Porthmadog. There are trains to Porthmadog from Pwllheli or Birmingham via Machynlleth on the scenic Cambrian Coast Line and a seasonal steam-hauled service on the Ffestiniog Railway from Blaenau Ffestiniog (linking with trains from Llandudno Junction). Buses stop right outside the Golden Fleece Inn, Tremadog. No 1 runs between Blaenau Ffestiniog and Caernarfon, no 2 links Aberystwyth, Dolgellau and Caernarfon, no 3 goes between Pwllheli and Blaenau Ffestiniog, while no 97 connects Porthmadog with Beddgelert. These provide a good weekday service and, with the exception of route no 1, a service on Sundays too.

The Golden Fleece Inn, Tremadog (0766 512421)

Breton onion sellers used to land their stock at Porthmadog, stay here with their Celtic cousins whose language is closely related to Breton and string their onions before departing on their bicycles. Real ale and food are available, as is bed and breakfast accommodation. There is a beer garden and opening hours are 11.30am to 2.30pm and 6pm to 11pm on weekdays (Dwyfor is 'dry' on Sundays, so this pub cannot open on a Sunday).

Tremadog

The Golden Fleece

A narrow vote in the House of Commons prevented nearby Porthmadog from becoming the ferry port to Ireland, instead of Holyhead. Tremadog is laid out as if it deserves to be the gateway to Wales and Snowdonia. It was built by A. W. Madocks in the early 19th century and is a fine example of a Regency town planned around a central square. Shelley wrote 'Queen Mab' here in 1812 and 1813, while T.E. Lawrence (Lawrence of Arabia) was born in what is now the Christian Mountain Centre in 1888.

Tremadog means Madocks' town, named after its builder. The legend of the Welsh Prince Madog ab Owain Gwynedd is also attached to it, although most experts reckon this explorer whose descendants may have been the so-called Welsh-speaking American Indian tribe known as the Mandans, set sail from near Colwyn Bay. Southey wrote a poem about the legend entitled Madoc. Porthmadog lost the Irish ferry but it did become an important port for the slate industry, connected with its hinterland by the Ffestiniog Railway, that can still take you to the slate town of Blaenau Ffestiniog. The Welsh Highland Railway also runs out of Porthmadog. Prehistoric men and women lived in huts on the hills above Tremadog and raised the standing stone seen on this route. As you approach Cae-glan-yr-afon, look ahead and to the right for a view of Snowdon, behind Moel Hebog.

The birthplace of Lawrence of Arabia

The Walk

1. Go right to pass St Mary's Church on your left and reach the Christian Mountain Centre on your left. This is where T.E. Lawrence (of Arabia) was born on 3rd April 1888. There is a small plaque on the building and a whitebeam tree was planted in the front garden to mark the centenary of his birth. Return towards the church and turn right along a signposted public footpath just before it. Follow the shaded path past woodland on your right and ignore a path going right through it.

2. Turn left at the corner of the wood to take a tree-lined path to the A498. Go left along its pavement. When you approach a garage, cross the road carefully and turn sharply right up a lane. Pass houses on your left, turn sharply left along a rough track above them and reach a tumbling stream on your right, level with the garage below on your left. Turn right uphill just after the stream. Reach a small gate in the fence above the wooded slope. Go ahead through it and up a walled track.

3. Reach the corner of a firm track and go straight ahead across a cattle grid. Approach Cwm Mawr farmhouse and bear left to cross a ladder stile beside a gate in the wall ahead. Climb to join a wall surmounted by a fence on your right.

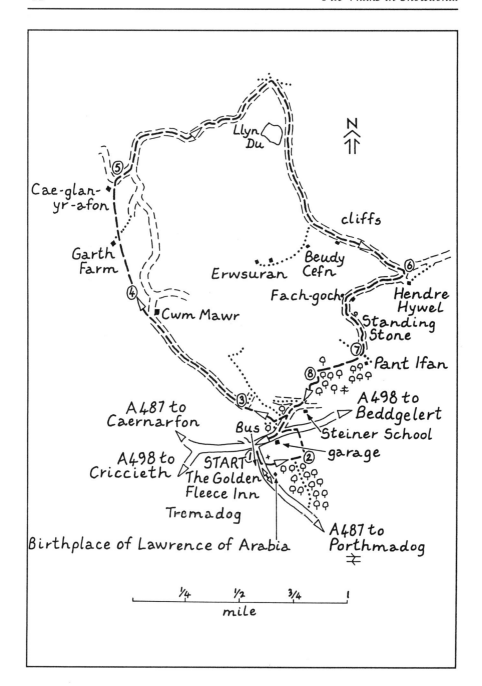

N

Llyn
Du

Cae-glan-
yr-afon

cliffs

⑤

Garth
Farm

④

Cwm Mawr

Erwsuran

Beudy
Cefn

Fach-goch

Hendre
Hywel

⑥

Standing
Stone

⑦

Pant Ifan

⑧

A487 to
Caernarfon

③

A498 to
Beddgelert

Bus

Steiner School

garage

A498 to
Criccieth

START

②

The Golden
Fleece Inn

Tremadog

A487 to
Porthmadog

Birthplace of Lawrence of Arabia

¼　　½　　¾　　1
mile

4. Bear right in the corner to cross the non-barbed wire fence and walk with a wall on your right to the next corner. Follow power lines to Garth Farm, which is passed on your left. Ignore a rough track going right. Take the field-gate ahead to maintain your direction to Cae-glan-yr-afon (used the ladder stiles in its fences, cross a stream by a footbridge and pass the house on your left). Reach a road where it makes a sharp bend.

5. Turn right along the road and bear left when a track joins it from your right. Follow the road, now a concrete lane, as it turns right to pass Llyn Du on your right. Pass the access track to Beudy Cefn and Erwsuran, then a cottage near the lane on your right. Reach a signposted public footpath on your right, above a farm and before the lane continues through a gate.

6. Turn sharply right down the signposted public footpath. This is a firm track which forks left down to the farm. Bear right at this fork to take a waymarked gate and continue past the farmhouse at Fach-goch. Notice a standing stone in the second field on your left after this house. The track bends right and takes a gate in a wall ahead.

7. Do not be tempted by the private path down to Pant Ifan on your left. Do take the narrow, waymarked, public footpath through bracken ahead. This soon forks right so that you walk with a wall on your left. Continue down a rocky valley fringed by trees. Turn left through a small metal gate and go down a wooded slope, made easier by a handrail and steps. Cross a stream and reach a stile in a fence.

8. Bear right to descend with a fence on your left. Emerge on a lane opposite Ysgol Steiner Eryri (Snowdonia's Steiner School – an independent school based on the principles of Rudolph Steiner). Don't take the uphill track that is immediately on your right. Do take the lower lane to go right back to Tremadog. Bear right at the A498 road, pass a garden centre on your left and reach the Market Square. The Golden Fleece Inn is ahead and on your left.

9. PLAS TAN-Y-BWLCH

Route: The Oakeley Arms Hotel, Maentwrog – Plas Tan-y-Bwlch – Rhyd – Llyn Mair – The Oakeley Arms Hotel, Maentwrog

Distance: 6 miles

Map: O.S. Outdoor Leisure 18 (Snowdonia – Harlech & Bala areas)

Start: The Oakeley Arms Hotel, Maentwrog (SH 660410)

Access: The Oakeley Arms is at the junction of the A487 and the B4410 about half a mile west of the A487's junction with the A496 at Maentwrog. Several buses stop right outside: Nos 1 (Blaenau Ffestiniog – Caernarfon), 2 (Aberystwyth – Dolgellau – Caernarfon), 3 (Blaenau Ffestiniog – Porthmadog – Pwllheli) and 38 (Blaenau Ffestiniog – Barmouth – Dolgellau).

The Oakeley Arms Hotel, Maentwrog (0766 85277)

Travellers on the notorious turnpike road between Caernarfon and Dolgellau took shelter in this pub during the 18th century. The section from Croesor to Maentwrog was known as 'the worst road in the Principality'. It was replaced by a new route now followed by the B4410 between Garreg and Maentwrog in 1812. The ghost of a lady regularly appears to guests, so if you are adventurous stay for bed and breakfast. Real ale and food are available and the film crew and cast of TV's Dr Who series left no complaints when they stayed here. Opening hours are 11am to 2.30pm and 6pm to 11pm on weekdays (11am to 11pm on Saturdays during the season), noon to 3pm and 7pm to 10.30pm on Sundays.

Plas Tan-y-Bwlch

This property came into the hands of William Oakeley from Staffordshire when he married into the Griffith family around 1785. The estate was a model of self-sufficiency in the 19th century with its 60 acres including a mill, tanneries, sawmill, smithy, church, shops, farms and two hotels. Rhododendrons were amongst the exotic plants brought to make its garden beautiful. The family's wealth came from the slate industry and the Ffestiniog Railway was built to service this. W G Oakeley (1790-1835) laid the first stone on the railway in 1833, at Creuau. He insisted on screening the railway with a wall where it came through his estate, however. The Oakeley's slate was transported by the Ffestiniog Railway at half the rate charged to other customers, while the family had their own private station (a special signal warned drivers to stop when required) and a special four-wheel open carriage. The last member of the Oakeley family, Mrs Inge, died in 1961 and the estate was acquired jointly by the Countryside Commission and the Snowdonia National Park Committee. Converted into a residential study centre, it opened in 1975. Many of the courses on offer feature some form of walking. For further details write to: Plas Tan-y-Bwlch, Maentwrog, Blaenau Ffestiniog, Gwynedd, LL41 3YU (tel: 0766 85324).

Many of the paths on this route are courtesy paths which are closed every year on 28th February. There are some superb views over the Vale of Ffestiniog, while the splendour of the scenery is matched by the delightful oak woodlands. The meandering river in the glacial valley below is the Afon Dwyryd. The Oakeley family built the embankments which control the river and drain the valley floor. Look out for dragonflies in the summer.

The Walk

1. Go right and fork left up the drive to Plas Tan-y-Bwlch. Round a hairpin bend and bear left along a woodland track to walk parallel to the drive. Go ahead through gates to pass along the top of the gardens and below the house. Where the path is blocked by a fence protecting a tree, follow the fence around to resume the path, then ascend steps on your right to gain the house's car park.

2. Take the signposted 'way out/ffordd allan' but after 20 yards, as the drive bends left, climb steps on your right, then bear left along a woodland path. Pass a greenhouse and potting shed on your left. Climb to walk parallel to but below the Ffestiniog Railway. Bear right to a ladder stile but do not cross it or the railway. Admire the view over the vale on your left, then go ahead through the woodland with the railway still on your right. Reach junction post 2.

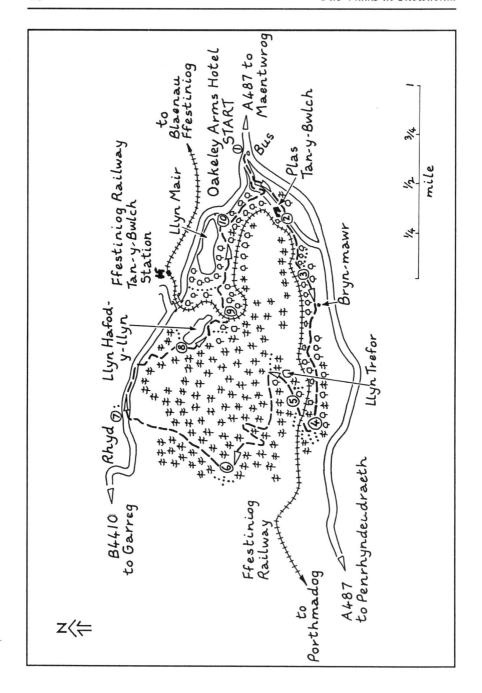

3. Ignore a path going left. Take the woodland path ahead. This gradually descends to pass Bryn Mawr on your left (heed the 'private' signs on its gates). Ascend with a wall on your left to regain contact with the railway. Keep within hailing distance of it on your right. Cross a stream and go ahead 25 yards to junction post 25.

4. Turn right up the waymarked ascending path. Take the gap in the wall ahead near junction post 24. Reach a wooden post with yellow and red arrows and turn right along the ascending path. Pass junction post 23 to reach the railway. Cross the line with care and climb with the woodland path to junction post 22.

5. Bear right along a wide, grassy, track. Ignore a path on your right at junction 21. Pass Llyn Trefor on your right. Reach a firm track and go left along it. Admire the view over the estuary on your left, round the corner on your right and fork left down the lower track. Round two hairpin bends as the track descends. Cross a stream to reach junction 34, where there is a waymarked path on your right. If you do overshoot, junction 35 is only 50 yards ahead, after the track crosses a second stream.

6. Turn right up the waymarked path. Climb through the forest to the top of the ridge. Ignore a track bearing right to old levels. Descend through the forest to a ladder stile in the perimeter wall. Continue up rough pasture with a wall on your right. Bear left as you approach a house. Take a gap in the wall to the left of it and descend to a kissing-gate beside a signpost which gives access to the B4410 road on the eastern side of Rhyd.

7. Turn right along the road to pass the house (Bron y Foel) on your right. Pass a signposted path going left. After a quarter of a mile, turn right along a signposted public footpath. This leads past trees to a wall. Do not go ahead through the gap in this wall. Turn left to walk with the wall on your right. Reach a firm track going around Llyn Hafod-y-Llyn (a reservoir).

8. Go right to walk with the lake on your left. Keep to the firm track overlooking the lake. Pass above the dam at the end of the lake, bear right and soon fork left down a grassy track. Cross the Ffestiniog Railway again, heeding warning notices.

9. Enter Woodland Trust land and follow a broad track to junction 27. Go right up a track and turn left at the next junction to take a gate and reach junction post 9. Fork left and descend to Llyn Mair on your left. Bear right along the lakeside track.

10. Fork right at junction post 11. Pass above a small lake on your left, then ignore the path bearing right at junction post 12. Keep to the main track to reach the Plas' drive. Turn left along it back to the Oakeley Arms Hotel.

The Oakeley Arms

10. GELLILYDAN

Route: The Bryn Arms, Gellilydan – Castell Tomen-y-mur – Trawsfynydd Nuclear Power Station – The Bryn Arms, Gellilydan

Distance: $5^1/_2$ miles (N.B. this route can be linked with that coming from Trawsfynydd to give a walk of $11^1/_2$ miles)

Map: O.S. Outdoor Leisure 18 (Snowdonia – Harlech & Bala areas)

Start: The Bryn Arms, Gellilydan (SH 685395)

Access: Gellilydan is just off the A487 near its junction with the A470, between Trawsfynydd and Ffestiniog. There is a bus stop in the village for Nos 2 (Dolgellau – Caernarfon) and 35 (Dolgellau – Blaenau Ffestiniog).

The Bryn Arms, Gellilydan (0766 85379)

This is more than a pub, it is a brewery. When publican Martin Barry started brewing his own real ale in 1992, he made this the only brewing pub in Wales. Barry's Brewery has been built inside the pub and customers can watch the entire process of their beer being made, from the mixing of the barley and the hops to the final pint in the pot. 'Mel y Moelwyn' (honey of the mountains) is a great favourite. A bitter beer, it is mildly hopped and has a taste of honey, while the water really does come from the mountains. A dry beer, it has an original gravity of 1039.

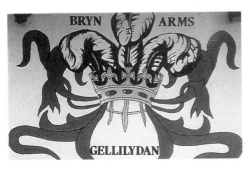

Barry also brews 'Snowdon' and 'Choir Porter'. Food is usually available in the summer, while camping may be possible. There is a Caravan Club site just across the road. Opening hours are usually only in the evenings, from 7pm to 11pm on weekdays, 7pm to 10.30pm on Sundays.

Trawsfynydd Nuclear Power Station

The Lake District has Sellafield and Snowdonia has Trawsfynydd. At least they didn't change the name. Sir Basil Spence (of Coventry Cathedral fame) designed the buildings but a glimpse of them is enough for most people to accept the presence of windmills and other less sinister forms of generating power.

In 1983 your author worked with Professor David Hall, an expert in solar energy from London University and a witness at the Windscale Inquiry, to produce a demonstration of bio-fuels, funded by the Vegan Society, at the Centre for Alternative Technology, just across the Afon Dulas from Snowdonia National Park, north of Machynlleth. Bio-fuels may help in restoring Snowdonia's natural vegetation, the sessile oak (alder is also a good bio-fuel, being high in calories). A coppiced forest could produce fuel on a renewable basis. Coppices provide habitats for wildlife, prevent soil erosion and oxygenate the air (to more than offset the carbon dioxide emissions).

The nuclear industry, on the other hand, uses admittedly proven technology which, nevertheless, does cause concern to some environmentalists. Make up your own mind by visiting the exhibition at Trawsfynydd Nuclear Power Station. There is even a glossy leaflet to nature rambles in the station's grounds. This is an ageing Magnox power station and the only nuclear power station in Britain to be built inland. It uses water from Llyn Trawsfynydd for cooling purposes. This lake was originally created as a reservoir in 1928 to supply water to the nearby Maentwrog hydro-electric station. Trawsfynydd's two reactors are each capable of meeting the demands of a city the size of Cardiff, and they started to supply electricity to the national grid in 1965. Irradiated fuel is sent in flasks by train to Sellafield and this has helped to keep the railway open from here to Llandudno Junction (passenger services run north from Blaenau Ffestiniog). If you would like a free tour of the nuclear power station, it is open daily (except for 25th and 26th December and 1st January) from 9.30am to 4.30pm. Tour times are usually at 10am, 11am, 1.30pm and 2.30pm. You are advised to pre-book by telephoning 0766 87622.

The Walk

1. Go left down the road to a junction before the bridge over the Afon Tafarn-helyg. Bear right along the lane signposted as a public footpath immediately before and to the right of the bridge. Pass cottages and follow a ridge path beside a fence on your right and above a stream on your left. Trawsfynydd Nuclear Power Station soon looms above the trees ahead.

2. Go ahead over a ladder stile, across the next field and through a gate. Continue over a stream and a waymarked slate stile in the wall to the right of a gate ahead. Bear slightly right through woodland to a ladder stile in the next wall. Follow a clear path, waymarked with painted yellow arrows on stones, through bracken and cross another ladder stile in the wall ahead. Negotiate a short boggy section (there are overhanging branches to cling to), cross a stream by the small slate bridge and reach a signposted junction with a firm track.

3. Turn left along the track to walk with a wall on your right. Pass the farm buildings of Ty Gwyn on your right. Reach the A470 and go left along its pavement for 100 yards. Turn right to cross the road carefully and follow an enclosed path which takes a footbridge over the railway. Ignore a field-gate ahead. Turn right to take the gate in the corner.

4. Walk along the foot of the field, with the fence on your right, for 100 yards. Turn left to walk up the field and pass a farm building on your right to go through a gateway. Bear right along the foot of the next field. This track marks the course of a Roman road (that from Caer Gai to Segontium). Continue over a stile and keep above a stream on your right for 300 yards. Gradually bear left uphill to a small gate in the fence on your right near a corner. Cross the following field to gain access to a road through a gate in its corner.

5. Go right along the road. This route turns right along the signposted public footpath opposite where a private road forks left.
IF YOU WISH TO LINK THIS ROUTE WITH THE ONE STARTING AT TRAWSFYNYDD, however, continue along the road to the next signpost, where the road bends left. This route crosses a footbridge

Continue over this stile on the old Roman Road (direction 4)

and a stile with the legend 'this footpath does not go to the fort'. It does go through the field ahead, to a waymarked stile in its far, top corner. The Roman fort (Castell Tomen-y-mur) is on your left.

6. Continue over the stile and with a fence on your right. The nuclear power station comes into view ahead, with Llyn Trawsfynydd on its

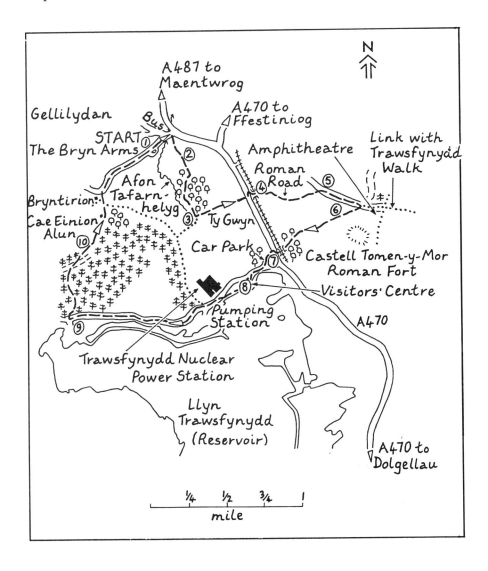

left. Take a gate in a corner near an electricity pylon and walk with a fence on your left down the next field. Go ahead over a stile below the power lines and follow a waymarked path through woodland down to a tunnel under the railway. Emerge to reach the A470.

7. Cross the road carefully and turn right along its pavement for about 50 yards, where the fence on your left ends. Turn left down a signposted public footpath. Take a gate ahead and follow a wide path towards the car park for visitors to the Nuclear Power Station. Take the pavement of the access road and use a zebra crossing to reach the Visitors' Centre.

8. Follow the start of the Gyfynys Trail, soon passing Lake View on your left and the picnic area on your right. Bear left through a waymarked gate to follow the lakeside path. Rejoin the road and go left along it. Ignore a fork bearing left to the pumping station. Keep to the road, ignoring a ladder stile in the fence on your right. Go ahead for one mile.

9. Notice a red 'Caution Footpath' road sign. Go ahead 75 more yards and turn right over a ladder stile to follow a signposted footpath through the forest. This soon bears right and is easy to follow to a track. Go right along this until it forks. Bear left along the lower, grassy track. Reach a stile beside a gate at the edge of the forest.

10. Go ahead under power lines and cross a ladder stile in the wall ahead near its corner with the perimeter wall of the forest on your right. Continue with a wall on your right to cross a ladder stile beside a gate in the next corner. Keep the wall on your right, cross a third ladder stile and bear left to Cae Einion Alun. Take its access track past Bryntirion to a road. Go right along this to pass Coed-y-llwyn caravan site on your right and reach the Bryn Arms on your left.

11. TRAWSFYNYDD

Route: The Cross Foxes Inn, Trawsfynydd – The White Lion, Trawsfynydd – Tomen-y-mur – Braich-ddu Quarries – Pant-mawr – The Cross Foxes Inn, Trawsfynydd

Distance: 6 miles (N.B. this route can be linked with that coming from Gellilydan to give a walk of $11^1/_2$ miles)

Map: O.S. Outdoor Leisure 18 (Snowdonia – Harlech & Bala areas)

Start: The Cross Foxes Inn, Trawsfynydd (SH 708356)

Access: Trawsfynydd is near the junction of the À470 with the A4212. There is a bus stop outside the Cross Foxes Inn for Nos 2 (Dolgellau – Caernarfon) and 35 (Dolgellau – Blaenau Ffestiniog).

The Cross Foxes Inn, Trawsfynydd (0766 87204)

The Hunt used to meet here, as did the drovers. So many horses would be attached to it that it became known colloquially as 'The Ring'. Singing is the pub's current attraction, with the Meibion Prysor male voice choir exercising their lungs here every Thursday night. They can't compete with the landlady (now Mrs Williams) who, as Edith Barker, sang with the group 'Pelydrau' on television's 'Opportunity Knocks' in the late 1960s. Bed and breakfast is available, as well as food and real ale. Opening hours are 11.30am to 4.30pm and 7pm to 11pm on weekdays, noon to 3pm and 7pm to 10.30pm on Sundays.

The White Lion Inn, Trawsfynydd (0766 87277)

This is another inn frequented by the drovers before the coming of the railway took away their livelihood. Real ale and bar meals are served, while bed and breakfast is available. Opening hours are noon to 3pm and 6pm to 11pm on weekdays, noon to 3pm and 7pm to 10.30pm on Sundays.

The statue of Hedd Wyn, Trawsfynydd

Hedd Wyn

Hedd Wyn was the bardic name of Ellis Humphrey Evans, the local boy who was also known as 'the shepherd poet'. Born on the 13th January 1887, he joined the Royal Welch Fusiliers in the first world war and was killed in action just before the result was announced of the poetry competition for the Chair at the 1917 National Eisteddfod. He won and that year's eisteddfod, held in Birkenhead, is remembered for the Chair being draped in black.

Tomen-y-mur

This is on private land, but the motte of a Norman castle (probably built by William Rufus on a campaign that was aborted because of the Welsh weather in 1095) is clearly visible. It stands within a fort built by the Romans in AD 78 and garrisoned until AD 140. Cavalry were based here until, perhaps, the last 20 years of the fort's use, when the garrison was reduced to an infantry unit. The initial turf and timber fort was later faced with stone, although the internal buildings, except for the bath house, don't seem to have been built of stone. This remote outpost of the Roman Empire boasted a level parade ground with ballista (siege-engine) platforms nearby. There was a small amphitheatre and 'practice camps' have been identified. The strategic importance of this site was its control of the roads. The name Trawsfynydd can be translated as 'across the mountain' and routes across the mountains met here. Sarn Helen, the road linking Carmarthen in south Wales with Caerhun (near Conwy) in north Wales crossed the road from Caer Gai (a Roman fort south of Bala) to Segontium (Caernarfon) here. This strategic nature must have held good during the so-called 'dark ages' when the story of *Math, son of Mathonwy* in *The Mabinogion* is set. This refers to a 'Mur Castell' as a stronghold of the chieftain of Ardudwy.

The Bala – Blaenau Ffestiniog Railway

From 1882 to 1961 this railway earned the reputation of being 'the wildest and most impressive hour of rail travelling in England or Wales'. It reached an altitude of 1200 feet at Cwm Prysor, just south of Trawsfynydd. Winter services were subject to disruption by snow. There are plans to turn the route into a walking trail.

The Walk

1. Go right to pass the statue of Hedd Wyn on your left and pass the White Lion on your right. Continue past Hedd Wyn's birthplace (marked by a plaque. on your right. Descend to the junction with the A470 and cross this road carefully.

2. Go straight ahead up an old green lane which starts between two walls. Don't take the first turning on your left down to a farm. Do go ahead through a gate and follow the wall on your left as it bears left. The wall is on your right in the next field, after which you turn right to climb stone steps in the wall. Turn left immediately to walk with the wall on your left. Descend to cross a stream.

3. Climb to a signpost and go ahead through a small wooden gate to walk with a wall on your left. Descend to a metalled lane. Bear left with it to a signpost and leave the lane to go ahead over a footbridge across Nant Islyn. Emerge on a lane near its junction with the A470.

4. Bear right along the lane, crossing the course of a dismantled railway. Fork left off the lane to follow a signposted public footpath. This is an old green lane which crosses a stream, continues through a gate and follows a wall on your left. Climb to pass under power lines ahead, passing the distinctive mound of Tomen-y-mur on your left. Bear left

across a stream and keep near the wall on your left. Go ahead to a signpost near the corner of a road on your left.

5. IF YOU WISH TO LINK THIS ROUTE WITH THAT FROM GELLI-LYDAN, go left along the road and bear left down the first signposted public footpath. CONTINUE THIS ROUTE by turning right along a firm track (as signposted). Pass a lake on your left, then the course of an old tramway on your right. After passing an old quarry the firm track becomes a grass path. Descend to a ruin and sheep-folds, where a stream flows on your left.

6. Ignore the course of the Roman road running down the valley on your right. Do not cross the stream on your left but do take the gate ahead. Turn left through the next gate, in the wall on your left, to cross the stream and climb with a wall on your left. Turn right to step across the stream above a waterfall. Continue under power lines, keeping to the left of the immediate pylon.

7. Cross the wall ahead by a stone step stile shortly after the stone wall resumes after nearly 100 yards of fencing coming from a stream on your left. Bear slightly left to join a firm track after 150 yards. Turn right along this.

8. Fork right as you approach buildings. Take a gate ahead and pass the lower house on your right. Follow the grass track ahead. This keeps close to the fence on your right. The fence switches to your left in the next field. Go ahead through three more gates and fields to reach Pant-mawr.

9. Follow the firm track from Pant-mawr to a road, which begins by crossing a bridge over the course of the dismantled railway. Go left up Stryd Ardudwy to a junction with a letterbox and turn right to the A470. Cross this road carefully and take the road ahead back into Trawsfynydd. The Cross Foxes is on your left, while the White Lion is on your right.

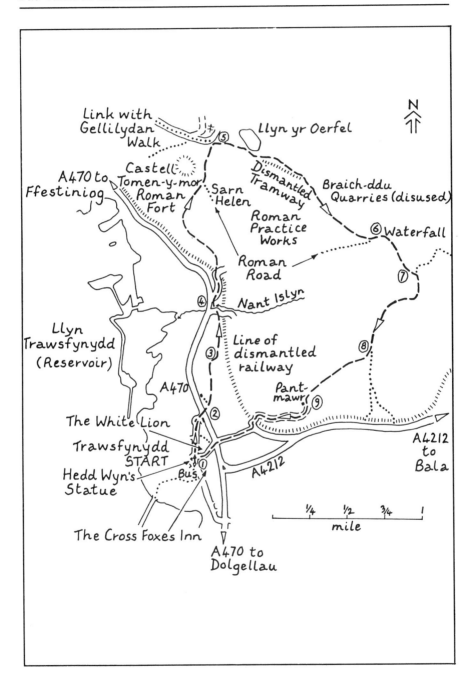

Link with Gellilydan Walk

Llyn yr Oerfel

Castell Tomen-y-mor Roman Fort

A470 to Ffestiniog

Sarn Helen

Dismantled Tramway

Braich-ddu Quarries (disused)

Roman Practice Works

Roman Road

⑥ Waterfall

⑦

Nant Islyn

④

Llyn Trawsfynydd (Reservoir)

Line of dismantled railway

③

⑧

A470

Pant-mawr ⑨

The White Lion

②

Trawsfynydd START

Hedd Wyn's Statue

Bus ①

A4212

A4212 to Bala

The Cross Foxes Inn

A470 to Dolgellau

¼   ½   ¾   1
mile

N

12. BALA LAKE (Llyn Tegid)

Route: The White Lion Royal Hotel, Bala – Bala Lake – Bala Lakeside Motel – Bryniau Goleu – Bryn-hynod – The White Lion Royal Hotel, Bala (optional return by steam-hauled train from Llangower)

Distance: $7^1/_2$ miles (or $5^1/_2$ miles if returning to Bala by train from Llangower)

Map: O.S. Outdoor Leisure 18 (Snowdonia – Harlech & Bala areas)

Start: The White Lion Royal Hotel, Bala (SH 926360)

Access: Bala is on the A494 between Dolgellau and Corwen. The No 94 bus which runs between Barmouth, Dolgellau, Corwen, Llangollen and Wrexham, stops in Bala High Street, near the start of this walk.

The White Lion Royal Hotel, Bala (0678 520314)

Queen Victoria once partook of afternoon tea here, hence the hotel's royal status. Marconi has also stayed here, There have been many other guests since the hotel opened its doors in 1759. Perhaps one lingers here as a ghost. The spectre of a woman has been seen by a guest in one of the bedrooms, while it was also witnessed by a former member of staff. Why not stay for bed and breakfast to see if the ghost will appear for you? If you're a vegetarian, you'll find there's no problem ordering a meal, while snacks are also available. Real ale is served and the bar opening hours are 11am to 11pm on weekdays, noon to 3pm and 7pm to 10.30pm on Sundays.

Bala

The first thing to sort out is how you are to complete this walk. The return along the road can be a bit tedious, but the idea is that you choose to go left when you drop down to it and take a train back to Bala from the Bala Lake Railway's station at Llangower. This friendliest of railways gives you a lakeside view and makes the perfect end to a scenic walk.

terminus at Llanuwchllyn, then return northwards to Bala. Trains run from April to October and timetable details are available if you telephone 0678 4666. Relax at a picnic place near the lake whilst waiting for the train in Llangower.

The White Lion Royal

The Bala Lake Railway (Rheilffordd Llyn Bala) celebrated its 21st anniversary in 1993, as well as the 125th anniversary of the line. There is a touch of sadness about this journey. It used to be a scenic pearl in British Rail's crown, with holiday trains from Manchester taking the tracks from Ruabon to Barmouth Junction (now called Morfa Mawddach on the surviving Cambrian Coast Line) that were dismantled in 1965. The present narrow gauge track was laid down in 1971. Four and a half miles of it link Llanuwchllyn and the former Bala Junction station. Bala's town station was to the north on the branchline to Blaenau Ffestiniog. It is worth recording that the author's wife regularly finds four-leaved clovers on the present Bala station, with 108 being picked one afternoon.

Turning our attention to the town at the start of this walk, admire the statue of Thomas Edward Ellis in Bala High Street. Born at Cynlas, near

The statue of Thomas Edward Ellis

Bala, in 1859, he graduated from Oxford University in 1884. He soon gained election as the Liberal M.P. for Merioneth, in 1886. The son of a tenant-farmer, rather than a landowner, he preceded David Lloyd George in really speaking for Wales. Education, Disestablishment, Land Reform and Home Rule were his platforms and he worked ceaselessly in the House to achieve these aims. He was made Junior Lord of the Treasury and Liberal Whip after the 1892 election, then Chief Whip in 1894. Severe illness had struck him down whilst in Egypt in 1890 and his life was tragically cut short in 1899 when he died at Cannes.

Bala might now be famous for Welsh whisky, but the town's Nonconformist conscience forced the distillery to close. Religion is strong here and it was the destination of Mary Jones' famous walk (see the route in this book from Abergynolwyn to Mary Jones' Cottage). There is a statue of the Rev. Thomas Charles (who gave Mary Jones his own Bible) outside Tegid Chapel. Charles' grandson, David Charles, was born in Bala and helped found a Calvinistic Methodist College here. It is now a Welsh Presbyterian Youth Centre. David Charles, too, has a statue.

This walk takes you to viewpoints above Bala Lake (Llyn Tegid). At four and a half miles in length and over half a mile in width, this is the largest natural lake in Wales. It was named after Tegid, who was drowned in the lake by his enemies. This was a really wicked thing to do as Tegid was a scholar who restored the ancient learning. There is something nasty stirring in the deep, however. A legendary evil king once lived in a palace where the lake is now. Vengeance came when his palace and the valley it stood in were flooded. Only an innocent harpist survived the inundation. Furthermore, there is a prediction that the lake will flood Bala and drown the Dee valley as far as Llanfor in the future.

Perhaps there's some special energy in the rift valley which contains the lake. Mysterious lights are seen in the sky around it on 5th January (old Christmas Day) and it has the Welsh version of the Loch Ness monster, called Teggy. The author happens to know the National Park warden who lives near the lake and witnessed a large body with eight dark feet of it showing above the water in the 1970s. Just to show what is possible, the lake is the sole habitat of the 'gwyniad'. This shy member of the salmon family has been trapped here since the end of the Ice Age.

The Walk

1. Take the pelican crossing over the High Street and go right towards Bala Lake. Pass Ye Olde Bulls Head on your left near the bus stop. Go ahead along the pavement of Pensarn Road (the old Roman road from Chester to Brithdir, where it joined Sarn Helen). Reach the Loch Cafe on your left.

2. Turn left along a signposted embankment path above the shore of Bala Lake, which is on your right. Ignore a signposted public footpath going left through a kissing-gate. Continue to a road and go right along it. Cross a bridge over the River Dee as it flows out of the lake. Go ahead over an old bridge (now for pedestrians only) and take the signposted path ahead for Bala lake Railway station. Take the footbridge across the railway.

3. Bear slightly right, as waymarked, over a field to the stile beside a gate in its corner. Continue over the stile and walk beside a hedge on your right. Take the gate in the corner and turn right along a track which passes conifer trees on your left. Ignore the signposted public footpath bearing left through these trees. Pass farm buildings on your right and continue above golf links. Pass the Bala Lakeside Motel and take the woodland path ahead when the hotel's drive curves right.

4. Pass above the golf course's bell and go ahead along the signposted path which runs beside a fence on your right, at the bottom of pasture. Keep above a house and follow the fence on your right. Cross a stream, continue over a stile when you reach a corner and bear left uphill to a rough lane (an unclassified county road). Cross this to climb with a hillside path to a ladder stile in a fence. Turn to admire the splendid view over Bala Lake.

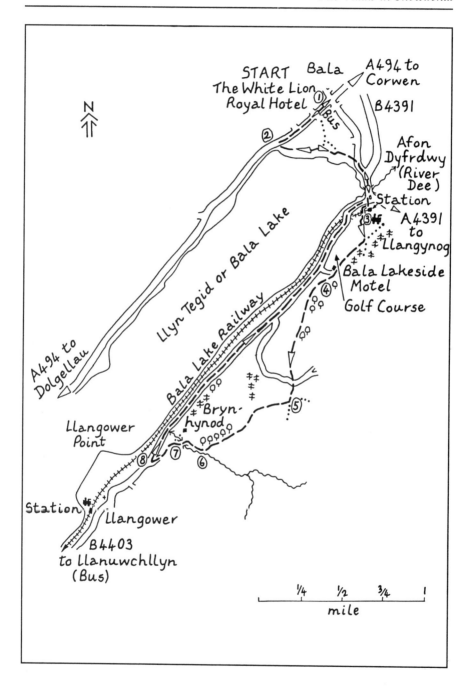

7. Go ahead along the signposted public footpath which soon converges with a fence on your left. There is a view of Moel y Garnedd across the lake on your right. Gradually descend to the road.

8. Either turn right to follow the road back to Bala (nearly all the traffic takes the A494 on the other side of the lake) OR turn left to follow the road to Llangower for the train back to Bala.

Bala Lake from the embankment path, Bala. Aran Benllyn is in the background

14|8|96   # *13. HARLECH*

Route: The Lion Hotel, Harlech – Coed Llechwedd – Lasynys-fawr – The Lion Hotel, Harlech

Distance: 4^1/$_2$ miles

Map: O.S. Outdoor Leisure 18 (Snowdonia – Harlech & Bala areas)

Start: The Lion Hotel, Harlech (SH 582312)

Access: The Lion is near the crossroads above the castle in the centre of Harlech, which is on the A496 from Dolgellau to Blaenau Ffestiniog via the Cambrian Coast. There is a car park near the bus stop (for Nos 38 and 94 running between Blaenau Ffestiniog and Dolgellau via Barmouth) not far from the Snowdonia National Park Visitors' Centre. Buses also stop near the railway station. Harlech is on the Cambrian Coast Line between Machynlleth and Pwllheli.

The Lion Hotel, Harlech (0766 780731)

David Lloyd George once stayed here, as have several famous golfers. Perhaps they enjoyed the Welsh singing late on a Saturday night. It wasn't always so. This was a Temperance hall in the 19th century, with The Lion pub housed next door. Food and real ale are served, while bed and breakfast accommodation is available. Opening hours are 11am to 11pm on weekdays, noon to 3pm and 7pm to 10.30pm on Sundays.

Harlech Castle

Harlech Castle has an incomparable natural setting, matched by the genius of its architect. It gives the impression of both power and beauty. The castle was built in the place associated with the legendary Branwen by the conquering English in 1283. Work started only six months after the death of Llywelyn the Last gave control of Wales to Edward I of England. Nearly 1000 men laboured on its construction over the next seven years, realising a single design.

This mighty fortress was a marvel of efficiency. Its permanent garrison consisted of only one constable, 'together with 30 fencible men of whom 10 shall be crossbow-men, one chaplain, an artiller, a smith, a carpenter and a mason. Master James of St George was brought from Savoy to direct the castle's construction and was appointed its first constable in 1290.

Harlech Castle

The castle was soon put to the test. Madog ap Llywelyn led the Welsh in an uprising in 1294 which saw Harlech cut off by land. In those days the sea came close to the castle and supplies were able to reach it by boat from Ireland. When Owain Glyndwr inspired the Welsh to fight for their independence again in the early 15th century, even the sea couldn't prevent Harlech Castle falling to him, in 1404. Harlech became his court and family home. The English didn't recapture it until very late in 1408 or early in 1409.

The famous song 'Men of Harlech' arose from the garrison's brave resistance to the Yorkists during the Wars of the Roses, during which time it gave shelter to Henry VI's queen, Margaret of Anjou. The damage sustained during this siege was never repaired. It was probably its remote position that made Harlech the last Royalist castle to surrender to the Parliamentarians in 1647. Cromwell didn't refrain from 'knocking it about a bit', but an order to demolish the castle was not carried out.

Today's ruins are well worth visiting. They are in the care of Cadw (Heritage in Wales). An excellent guidebook is available to this official World Heritage Site which is open daily except on Christmas Eve, Christmas Day, Boxing Day and New Year's Day. Opening hours are 9.30am to 6.30pm on weekdays (4pm in winter), 2pm to 6.30pm on Sundays (4pm in winter).

The Walk

1. Go right uphill and soon fork left along a lane to overlook the castle on your left. Bear left along a track between a chapel on your left and a cemetery on your right. Fork left off the track along the narrow public footpath which emerges at a signpost near a junction with a private road which descends on your left.

2. Go straight ahead along the signposted public footpath, passing below a house on your right. Continue through two small metal gates and past a signposted junction with a path descending from your right. Descend through the Woodland Trust's Coed Llechwedd to the B4573 road.

3. Go right along the road for half a mile. About 25 yards before there is a 'Croeso/Welcome to Harlech' sign on your right, bear left over a slate step stile in the wall and descend through woodland. Meet a wall on your left and go ahead over a fence (not difficult, but a stile has been requested) near its corner with the wall. Step across a muddy stream at the foot of the wooded slope.

4. Go ahead along the foot of the wooded slope to the corner ahead where there is a waterfall on your right. Turn left to follow the fence on your right. Take the gate in the next corner, on your right, to walk along the left hand edge of the next meadow. Go ahead through the gate in its corner and bear left immediately through another gate. Continue over the next meadow to Lasynys, which was clearly once an island. Take a gap in its wall and go right to walk with the wall on your right.

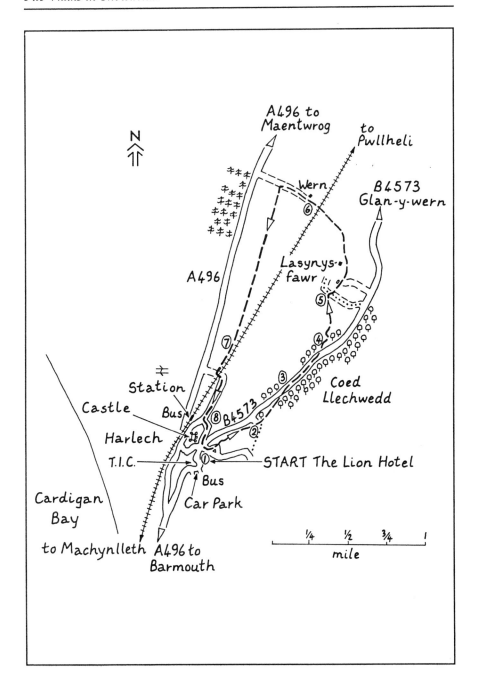

5. Cross a farm access lane. Reach a gate in a corner on your left. Take it and a subsequent footbridge formed by an old door. Pass a ruined farmhouse on your left and go through a gate between its wall and an outbuilding to continue along a walled track. When this bears left to the new farm buildings of Lasynys-fawr, do not take the field-gate ahead but do bear right through the gate in the same fence 50 yards to its right. Cross this field diagonally to a gate in its far corner. Go left through it to walk with a stream on your right to the railway line, which must be crossed very carefully.

6. Take the old green lane ahead to pass a farm (Wern) on your right. Look for a stile in the fence on your left, just before the lane crosses a stream. Turn left to walk with the stream on your right. Harlech Castle is a clear target on the horizon ahead and a series of stiles leads towards it. Reach a gate giving access to the railway but do not go through it!

7. Walk towards Harlech with the railway on the other side of the fence on your left. Reach a lane and, heeding the warning notices, turn left to cross the railway. Bear right along the road which passes a junior school and a fire station on your right.

8. Turn left up a No Through Road to pass Woodlands Caravan Park on your right. Climb to pass the castle on your right and reach the crossroads in the centre of Harlech. The Lion Hotel is straight ahead.

14. LLANUWCHLLYN

Route: The Eagle's Inn, Llanuwchllyn – Cefn-gwyn – Aran Benllyn – Coed-y-pry – The Eagle's Inn, Llanuwchllyn

Distance: $6^1/_2$ miles

Map: Both O.S. Outdoor Leisure 23 (Snowdonia – Cadair Idris area) and O.S. Outdoor Leisure 18 (Snowdonia – Harlech & Bala areas) are necessary

Start: The Eagle's Inn, Llanuwchllyn (SH 873303)

Access: Llanuwchllyn is at the junction of the A494 and the B4403 near the southern end of Bala Lake (Llyn Tegid). Bus No 94 runs from Barmouth via Dolgellau and from Wrexham via Bala. The Bala Lake Railway provides a delightful seasonal steam train service along the shore of Bala Lake from Bala (tel: 0678 4666 for timetable details).

The Eagle's Inn (Tafarn yr Eryred), Llanuwchllyn (0678 4278)

A warm welcome awaits you in this converted farmhouse. The food is tempting, the ale is real and the service is swift and courteous. Opening hours are 11.30am to 3pm and 6pm to 11pm on weekdays, noon to 3pm and 7pm to 10.30pm on Sundays.

Llanuwchllyn

The heart of Welsh language, culture and nationalism beats more strongly here than elsewhere in the Principality. Speak not of survival. The word here is resurgence. some of the greatest Welsh patriots and advocates of the Welsh language have been born here.

Michael Daniel Jones was born in the Manse, Llanuwchllyn, in 1822. The son of the Independent minister of Yr Hen Gapel, he followed in his father's footsteps by becoming a minister. A trip to America led him to promote the establishment of a Welsh colony, aiming to keep Welsh emigrants together so that they could preserve their national identity and language. He laboured to realise his vision in Patagonia, where his son Llwyd ab Iwan was murdered. At home he became the Principal of the College in Bala (it later moved to Bangor) and fought against the oppressive Tory landlord Sir Watkin Williams Wynn.

The Eagle's Inn

Coed-y-pry, a farmhouse that can be seen across the valley at point 6 on this walk, was the birthplace in 1858 of Owen Morgan Edwards. A well-loved scholar, he suffered from the iniquitous practice of 'Welsh Not' in the village National school, where he became a pupil teacher. Any child caught speaking Welsh, either during lessons or in the school playground, was made to wear a sign saying 'Welsh Not' until he could detect another child speaking Welsh. The one with the sign at the end of the day was punished. That's how the English tried to destroy the Welsh language. He went on to Bala's Calvinistic Methodist College, the

University College of Wales, Aberystwyth, Glasgow University and Balliol College, Oxford, where he began an outstanding career in 1885.

After spending a year travelling around continental Europe, he was elected Fellow and Tutor at Lincoln College, Oxford in 1889. Remaining there until 1907 and being recognised as an Honorary Fellow for the rest of his life, he gained a great reputation as a lecturer and tutor. He helped found the Dafydd ap Gwilym Society, a University club which conducts its affairs entirely in the Welsh language. He could have had a long parliamentary career, being returned unopposed to the House of Commons as Liberal member for Merioneth after the death of Tom Ellis in 1899. He chose not to stand at the forthcoming General Election, however, although he had a 'safe' seat.

As a historian, he preferred the vision of the artist to the dry bones of a researcher. He wrote for the common man and woman, popularising history and literature in both Welsh and English. He became joint-editor of *Cymru Fydd*, resigning when it became too political, then started the monthly journal *Cymru* in 1891. A monthly magazine for children, *Cymru'r Plant*, followed in 1892. He continued to edit both for the rest of his life. The quarterly *Y Llenor* was founded in 1895, while he also edited *Wales*, a magazine for non-Welsh-speaking people in the Principality. He gained a reputation as a helpful, considerate, editor who discovered much new talent. He wrote popular books and provided the Welsh people with cheap reprints of their classic literature. He also wrote the volume on Wales in English in the Story of the Nations series. He advised on the granting of charters to the University of Wales and was appointed Chief Inspector of Education in Wales in 1907. He enthusiastically inspired others to teach the language and culture of Wales. He loved nature rather than politics, was knighted in 1916 and died at Llanuwchllyn in 1920.

Sir Owen's son, Sir Ifan ab Owen Edwards, founded the first all-Welsh school in 1939. He'd already started the Urdd Gobaith Cymru (Welsh League of Youth) in 1922, when he was 27. A non-political and non-sectarian Youth movement, the Urdd 'believes that all Welshmen, whether Welsh-speaking or not, can grow to full stature and contribute to the welfare of the peoples of the world only by having their roots in their own historical tradition, and inheriting that wonderfully rich culture of the democracy that is Wales'. Sir Ifan ab Owen Edwards died in

1970 and a statue of him and his father can be seen at the junction of the A494 with the B4403.

Aran Benllyn is ascended by a series of terraces. The ridge is like a spine running from the foot of the mountain to its 2901 feet summit. With nothing to obscure the view, admire Snowdon, Arenig Fawr (2800 feet) and Bala Lake. King Arthur was brought up at nearby Caer Gai with his foster-brother Sir Cai and slew the giant Rhita Gawr in this region (as he followed the road over Bwlch y Groes) when the giant demanded his beard. Rhita's grave is here (and not on Snowdon).

Approaching the 2901' summit of Aran Benllyn

The Walk

1. Go left to pass St Deiniol's church on your left. Follow the pavement of the B4403, cross the Afon Dyfrdwy (River Dee) and pass a signposted public footpath between the public toilets and the chapel on your left. Turn right through a gate shortly after it to follow a signposted public footpath on your right. Walk with a fence on your left for 50 yards to a stile in it.

2. Bear left over the stile and walk along the left-hand edge of this field, towards Aran Benllyn's peak. Take the gap into the next field and continue along its left-hand edge to reach a lane. Go right along this.

3. Bear left to cross the course of the dismantled railway that connected Llanuwchllyn with Dolgellau. Fork right and cross a cattle grid. Follow the lane past a bungalow called Derwen Gam on your right, soon followed by the farmhouse of Cil-gellan on your left. The lane deteriorates to a grass strip between two narrow concrete corridors. Pass the farm buildings of Cefn-gwyn on your left. The route between here and the Arans ridge path is not the line of the right of way as shown on the O.S. map. This route is waymarked and has the necessary stiles, however. Efforts are being made to divert the right of way along it so that the maps can be a correct guide to the route actually walked on the ground. Access is a very sensitive issue on the Arans, so do keep to the waymarked path and please don't bring a dog!

4. Follow the waymarked route which goes over a ladder stile in the fence on your left. Keep to the waymarked path which climbs to join a fence, becoming a wall, on your left. Go ahead over a ladder stile in the corner and take the waymarked path over the moorland, ignoring the bridleway running beside the wall on your left. Cross a ladder stile ahead to reach the courtesy path which runs along the Arans ridge. Turn right along it to climb to the 2901 feet summit of Aran Benllyn. Navigation is made easy by the accompanying fence. Pass a small lake (Llyn Pen Aran) as you approach the peak, which is marked by a cairn of stones.

5. Retrace your steps down the Arans ridge path. Bala Lake is easy to

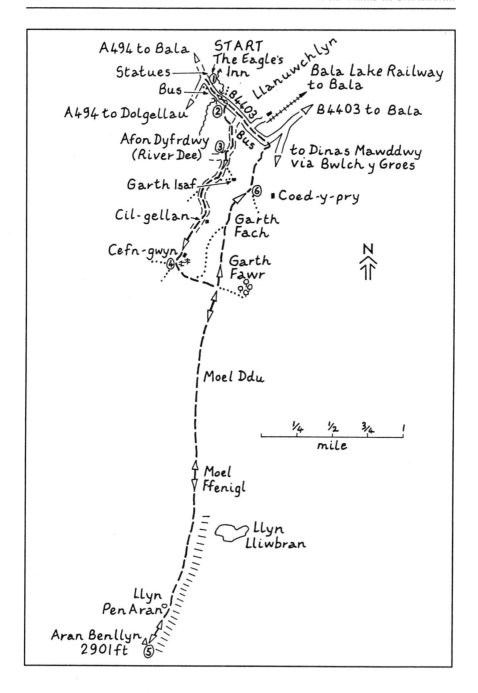

spot in front of you, but look east (to your right) on the highest stage to see Lake Vyrnwy in the distance. The lake immediately below the crags on your right is Llyn Lliwbran. When you return to the point where you first joined the ridge path, notice the wooded hollow on your right. This is where Sir Owen Morgan Edwards built himself a retreat whilst on holiday from Oxford. Although left as a ruin, it still has its corrugated roof and the window frames have survived well. Owen liked to meditate and reach into his imagination here. A Bronze Age axe was found in the neighbouring field, so prehistoric man knew this area. Continue down to a ladder stile beside a public bridleway signpost at its junction with the valley track.

6. Your way down to Llanuwchllyn goes left down the metalled track. Before taking it, however, notice the home of Sir Owen Morgan Edwards, Coed-y-pry, across this valley. Notice too the ruin on this side of the track a little to your right, which is all that remains of a 'ty unos', or one-night house. Welsh tradition allowed for a person to erect a roof of his house in a single night, with the smoke of a fire escaping through its chimney. He could then claim all the land within an area defined by throwing an axe in the four cardinal points of the compass. Later, his neighbours would help him to construct a more substantial house. Descend with the metalled track to Llanuwchllyn where you turn left along the B4403. Pass a bus shelter on your left and the access road to the Bala Lake Railway station on your right. Continue along the pavement of the B4403 back to the Eagle's Inn, on your right. Extend this walk by continuing past the pub, pass the old village pump on your right and reach the statues of Sir Owen Morgan Edwards and his son Sir Ifan ab Owen Edwards at the junction of the B4403 with the A494. Retrace your steps to the pub.

15. CWM NANTCOL

Route: The Victoria Inn, Llanbedr – Dolmygliw – Capel Salem – Foel Ddu – Maes-y-garnedd – Cwm Nantcol – Coed Aberartro – The Victoria Inn, Llanbedr

Distance: 10 miles

Map: O.S. Outdoor Leisure 18 (Snowdonia – Harlech & Bala areas)

Start: The Victoria Inn, Llanbedr (SH 585269)

Access: Llanbedr is on the A496 between Barmouth and Harlech. The No 38 bus from these two places stops near the start of this walk, while Llanbedr has a halt on the Cambrian Coast Line (Machynlleth – Pwllheli) half a mile to the west of the centre of the village, where the Victoria Inn is.

The Victoria Inn, Llanbedr (0341 23213)

Originally called The Goat, this old coaching inn has become expert at catering for tourists. This is a Robinson's house, incorporating Hartley's. Traditional ales are a speciality, including Old Tom, a famous winter warmer that has been brewed continuously since 1899. It has a flavour richly redolent of the malted barley, is the colour of wine and has no less than 8.5% alcohol. By contrast, Wheelwright is a recently introduced beer with less than 1% alcohol content. It has a full flavour coming from malt and hops, with no artificial colourings, flavourings, preservatives or sweeteners. Both are available on draught or in bottles. The food is good too, with vegetarians and vegans catered for. Fresh vegetables come from the inn's own market garden. Stay for bed and breakfast (there are bargain weekend breaks). Children will enjoy the Wendy House, slides and swings in their play area. Bar opening hours are 11am to 11pm on weekdays, noon to 3pm and 7pm to 10.30pm on Sundays.

The Victoria Inn

Llanbedr

The local standing stones are worth seeing, as is an unusual stone carved with a spiral and housed in the parish church. They feature on a short walk from the village in another book published by Sigma Press: *Welsh Walks: Dolgellau and the Cambrian Coast* by Laurence Main and Morag Perrott. The Victoria Inn, Llanbedr, may have copies of this guidebook for sale at £5.95.

Capel Salem

This isolated Baptist chapel acquired fame and notoriety when the Devon artist Sydney Curnow Vosper painted a picture in it in 1908. Reckoned to be the most famous painting of a Welsh scene, it shows the interior of the chapel and features an old lady, Sian Owen, in a shawl, with hymn book or Bible in hand. Unfortunately, this epitome of a Welsh mother has the devil's countenance traced in her shawl. At least it is easy to see when pointed out to you. Some say only those with evil in their hearts can spot it first time. The artist never admitted to including the devil in his painting. He merely wished to record for posterity a typical Welsh scene that was about to disappear with the loss of faith in rural Wales. It is a sad fact that the Paisley shawl was not Sian's own humble one, which she does wear in another Vosper painting, *Market Day in Old Wales*. The steeple hat is also out of place.

Vosper did use considerable artistic licence. Not one of the ladies in the painting owned a hat. The same one was shared between them, borrowed from the grandmother of Rev. Evan Rowlands (to the fashion of whose day it belonged). The six-year-old boy sitting beside his aunt was actually given a Quaker Oats box to hold, in case he was tempted to turn the pages of a real hymn book. Apples, oranges and chocolate were placed on the book ledge in front of him to entice him to sit still. The effective simplicity and sincerity of Vosper's work is evident in the swing of the pendulum, conveying the momentum of the clock. The picture was painted only four years after the great 1904 Revival. It portrays the virtues of Non-conformism, symbolised by the book in Sian Owen's hand. Did he also intend it as a cunning caricature of Welsh piety and hypocrisy? The argument made the painting known throughout the land but poor old Sian, who was 71 at the time of the painting, had to live with it until she died at the age of 90. Strangely, she was not buried here but in Llanfair. Her tombstone reads 'I am afflicted above measure: give me life, O Lord, according to Thy Word' (Psalms 119:107).

Salem was exhibited at the Royal Academy in 1909 and bought later that year by the first Lord Leverhulme for one hundred guineas. Copies of the painting were presented to people who bought quantities of Sunlight soap. Large numbers of prints were distributed by the Urdd (Urdd Gobaith Cymru – Welsh League of Youth) from 1937. It also featured as the cover of the *Cymru Fydd* calendar in 1950, 1956 and 1957. The Welsh Channel Four (S4C) television programme *Hel Straeon* came up with a second, slightly different, original of this painting in 1988. Vosper had painted it for his brother-in-law, a Merthyr Tydfil solicitor. If you want to see the original, visit the Lady Lever Art Gallery in Port Sunlight. The other *Salem* (painted as a half-size replica) has been inherited by a Worcester lady.

Go through this gate. Rhinog Fach (2333') is in the background.

Maes-y-garnedd

Nestling in the hollow of picturesque Cwm Nantcol is the farmhouse of Maes-y-garnedd. This is where Sian Owen, the dominant figure in the painting, was born in 1837. As was the current custom, she was brought up by her uncle, at Llwyn Hwlcyn, near Llanfair. This farm has a greater historical connection, however. It was the home of Colonel John Jones (1597-1660). He too achieved fame and notoriety. As the eldest son, he was sent to London to earn his fortune. A lawyer, he also became an officer in the Parliamentary army in the Civil War. He became MP for Merionethshire in 1647 and a member of the Court of Justice the next year. Now a judge, he was fated to be the first to sign King Charles I's death warrant in 1649. In 1656 he married his second wife, Katherine, the sister of Oliver Cromwell. The following year he was made Lord Jones and became Commissioner for Ireland. all this glory only led to his arrest on a charge of treason at the Restoration in 1660. He was executed as a regicide in London on 17th October 1660. Perhaps it is the shape of the land around here that produces such characters. Look around you at the peaks of Rhinog Fawr (2362 feet), Rhinog Fach (2333 feet) and Y Llethr (2475 feet).

The Walk

1. Go left to cross the bridge over the Afon Artro. Turn left immediately along the signposted public footpath which begins by running upstream beside the river on your left. Continue with a hedge on your left and past a football pitch on your right. Take the waymarked kissing-gate in the corner and turn right to walk with the hedge now on your right. Reach a farmyard and turn left through a gate to follow its access lane which rises above the river on your left.

2. Reach a signposted junction with a lane, bear left along this to keep above the river on your left. Bear left when the lane forks. Follow it through delightful woodland, ignoring a signposted public footpath on your right. Pass the farmhouse at Dolmygliw, after which the lane becomes a riverside path. Turn left over a footbridge to reach a road.

3. Go right along the road, above the river on your right. Bear right at a junction to take a bridge over the river. Turn left to follow a lane

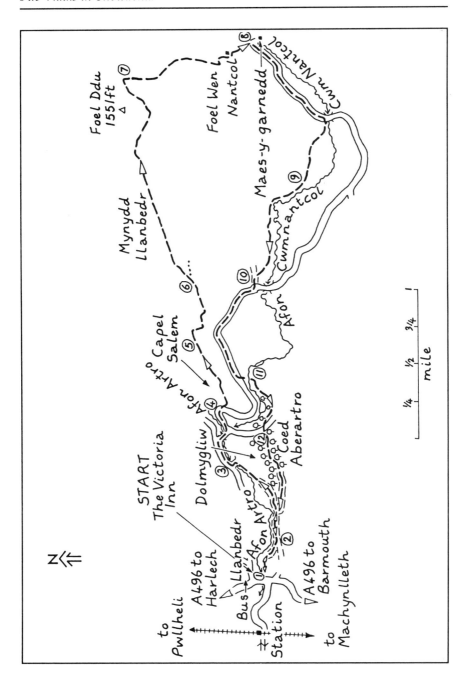

which starts with a cattle grid. This is signposted for Cwm Nantcol and Capel Salem. Walk up a wooded valley with the river on your left. Reach Capel Salem on your left.

4. Ignore the signposted public footpath on your left immediately after Capel Salem. Bear left shortly after along the next signposted public footpath. This soon becomes a grassy track beside dry stone walls. Turn left with the track to a gap in the far wall beneath a tree. Follow the track through to a gap and pass enclosed land, referred to by explanatory notices of a Farm Trail. Maintain your direction through a gateway into the next field. Cross a ladder stile in its far corner.

5. Veer very slightly right to pass close to a farmhouse on your right. Go down its concrete drive, then turn right uphill at a waymarked path junction. follow a steep, walled, old drovers' track. Bear left with this in a corner to emerge in an open field strewn with boulders. Go right along a grassy track which soon turns left to resume your former direction.

6. Bear left when the grass track forks and follow it to a gate in the top corner of the field. Go ahead through this and the next gate, keeping close to the wall on your right. Take a gap in the corner ahead and follow the track as it diverges from the wall before returning to go through a gate in the far corner. Contour around Foel Ddu at a height of about 1300 feet above the sea which affords a magnificent view when looking back. Suddenly Rhinog Fawr (2362 feet) is ahead of you. Rhinog. Fach (2333 feet) and Y Llethr (2475 feet) are on your right. Reach a corner and take the gap in the wall on your right.

7. Turn right to veer slightly left below the wall on your right and reach a ladder stile in the wall ahead. Cross it and continue down to take a gate in the next wall. Go ahead along a grassy track which is soon joined by a wall on your left. Eventually the path goes left through a gate in the wall to descend to Nantcol farmhouse. A walled access track leads down to the lane above Maes-y-garnedd.

8. Go right along the lane. As you approach a bridge over a river, turn right along the signposted public footpath which crosses a field to a gate in the wall opposite. Continue around the hillside above the river on your left, soon bearing right through a gap in a wall. Pass

gorse bushes and take the gap in the next wall. The narrow but obvious path traverses some rough terrain before joining a wall on your left and coming to a ruin.

9. Go ahead across the stone stile in the corner of the wall and continue over the ladder stile in the fence after it. Pass a footbridge on your left and walk with the river on your left, ignoring inviting planks to step across tributaries on your right. Go ahead over a footbridge in the corner to keep roughly parallel to the river on your left. Cross bridges over tributary streams to take the ladder stile in the fence ahead. Join a wall on your right, go ahead over a ladder stile beside a gate in the wall ahead to reach a lane.

10. Go left along the lane. Reach a junction with a road and go right to follow it for one mile. Continue over a cattlegrid, then turn left down a signposted public footpath. Cross a metalled track go through a patch of woodland and take the footbridge ahead to cross the river.

11. Bear right to walk above the river on your right, following power lines. Follow the green track through more woodland and above a shaded reservoir on your right. Continue through a gate and past fields on your left. Take the next gate to enter Coed Aber Artro (the Woodland Trust), resplendent with a carpet of bluebells in May. Cross a road.

12. Continue along the signposted woodland path which eventually comes to a gate. Go through this to join a rough lane at a signpost and go right. Follow the rough lane as it bends left through the woodland to the fork encountered on your outward route. Retrace your steps as you go ahead back to Llanbedr.

16. PONT-SCETHIN

Route: Ysgethin Inn, Talybont – Gors-y-Gedol Burial Chamber – Pont-Scethin – Llyn Erddyn – Ysgethin Inn, Talybont

Distance: 8 miles

Map: O.S. Outdoor Leisure 18 (Snowdonia – Harlech & Bala areas)

Start: The Ysgethin Inn, Talybont (SH 591218)

Access: Talybont is on the A496 between Barmouth and Harlech. The No 38 bus from these two places stops near the start of this walk. Talybont also has a halt on the Cambrian Coast Line (Machynlleth – Pwllheli)

The Ysgethin Inn, Talybont (0341 247578)

This was originally a fulling mill or pandy, although part of the building may have served as an inn when it opened on 1st February 1788. The pandy was replaced by a woollen factory in 1880, then the whole building became an inn in the 1930s. A Pelton Wheel from the 19th century pandy can still be seen. The nearby Rural Life Museum will show you more things of the past (tel: 0341 247690 for opening hours). Real ale and food are served in the pub, which features an inglenook and a bread oven. A ghost has often been heard by the staff but you might be the first to actually see it! There is a family room and a play garden. Bar opening hours are 11am to 3pm and 6pm to 11pm on weekdays, noon to 3pm and 7pm to 10.30pm on Sundays.

Gors-y-Gedol Burial Chamber

Also known as Arthur's Quoit, this burial chamber with its impressive capstone is near hawthorn bushes on your left as you walk from Llety Lloegr. It is most likely a reminder of the time when people came here from Ireland, when, indeed, the Irish Sea was narrower and shallower. Hut circles in this area are known as 'cyttiau gwyddelod', or Irishmen's huts.

Gors-y-Gedol burial chamber

Pont-Scethin

This remote structure became one of the most famous bridges in Wales when Fay Godwin, erstwhile president of the Ramblers' Association, took a superb photograph of it which adorns the cover of her book (with text by Shirley Toulson): *The Drovers' Roads of Wales* (Whittet Books 1987). It is a surprising sight, being a substantial bridge in a wild, remote spot. It wasn't built to accommodate even the most heavily-laden backpacker. It marks where an old drovers' road crossed the Afon Ysgethin. It also took the London mail coach from Harlech. The cattle were shod at Lletty Lloegr, which means English Shelter and was an overnight stop on the drove road to England at this walk's direction point 3.

The Walk

1. With your back to the pub, go right to pass the Rural Life Museum on your left. Reach the riverbank and ignore the footbridge on your

right. Walk upstream, soon taking a small metal gate ahead. Pass a second footbridge on your right (this is the one you will return over at the end of this walk). Follow the main path through the woods as it diverges from the riverbank.

2. Go ahead over a ladder stile beside a gate when you reach a fence in the woods. Continue over a small footbridge across a tributary stream. Climb steps and ignore the track which goes sharply left at a junction. Go ahead to keep above the river on your right. Ignore a second sharp turning to your left and stay above the river on your right.

3. Reach a metalled lane at Lletty Lloegr and go left along it (the old drovers' road). This route is even more ancient than the drovers for you pass the prehistoric burial chamber on your left. Continue through a gate to a junction and turn right to take a firm, walled, track through another gate with a Snowdonia National Park sign stating 'Dim cerbydau tu hwnt i'r pwynt yma' (No vehicles beyond this point). Follow the track, which may be used by Water Board vehicles, for over two miles.

4. Fork right when you notice a yellow arrow on a waymark post and a Welsh Water/Snowdonia National Park sign stating that this is a reseeded area, please keep to the waymarked path (*tir wedi ail-hadu, cadwch at y llwybr sydd wedi ei arwyddo, os gwelwch yn dda*). Follow this waymarked path to Pont-Scethin, the remote bridge.

5. Cross Pont-Scethin and follow the waymarked path which soon bears right to cross a boggy patch with the aid of planks, then bears left. At the end of the reseeded path, fork right down the valley. Follow a grassy track for about three miles, going through several gates in walls ahead. Pass a lake (Llyn Erddyn) on your left. Bear left when the track forks. Eventually, walk with a wall on your right to reach a T junction with another track (both old drovers' roads).

6. Turn left up the track to walk with a wall on your right. Fork right to keep above the wall as it turns. Go ahead through a gate in the corner. Pass farm buildings on your left and a farmhouse on your right. Take the walled grass track ahead. Bear left to pass another farmhouse on your right, making sure you turn right in its yard, rather than careering ahead along its access track!

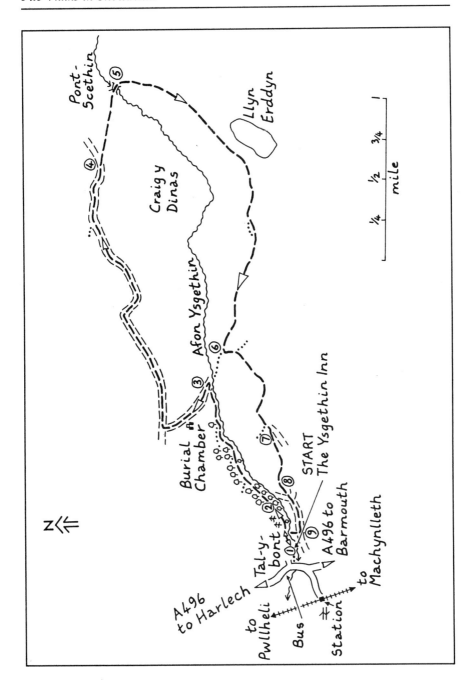

7. The right of way takes a gate in the far left corner of the farmyard and continues between stone walls, then across an open area fringed by trees. Go over a stone step stile in the wall ahead (ignoring a small metal gate in the wall on your left). Cross a field to the gate in a wall opposite. Continue through it and with a wall on your right in the next field. This bears right so that you walk with the wall on your left in the following field.

8. Continue through a gate in the corner and beside a wall on your left, above a wooded river valley on your right. Ignore a track going down to a farm on your right. Go ahead to a lane and bear right along it for about a quarter of a mile.

9. Turn right at a public footpath signpost to follow an enclosed path to the footbridge noted on your outward route. Cross it and turn left to retrace your steps to the pub.

The Ysgethin Inn

17. COED Y BRENIN

Route: Ty'n-y-groes Hotel – Pont – Cefndeuddwr – Gwynfynydd Gold Mine – Pistyll Cain – Ty'n-y-groes Hotel

Distance: 9^1/$_2$ miles

Map: O.S. Outdoor Leisure 23 (Snowdonia – Cadair Idris area)

Start: Ty'n-y-groes Hotel (SH 728232)

Access: Ty'n-y-groes Hotel is beside the A470 one mile out of Ganllwyd and four miles north of Dolgellau. As well as the parking spaces on the side of the hotel, there is a car park near the bridge over the Afon Mawddach as this walk enters Coed y Brenin. Ty'n-y-groes Hotel is a request stop for buses Nos 2 (Aberystwyth – Dolgellau – Maentwrog – Caernarfon) and 35 (Dolgellau – Blaenau Ffestiniog).

Ty'n-y-groes Hotel (0341 40275)

This old drovers' inn dates from at least the 16th century. It acquired its resident ghost relatively recently when a little girl was knocked down in a traffic accident outside. She was taken up to a bedroom (no 2) but expired there. Later, a man staying in that room reported being disturbed by what appeared to be her ghost. Staff also find the mirrors in that room are interfered with somehow. You can stay in this or another room on a bed and breakfast basis. Real ale is served, while food is available. Opening hours are 11am to 3pm and 7pm to 11pm on weekdays, noon to 3pm and 7pm to 10.30 pm on Sundays.

Coed y Brenin

Coed y Brenin means The King's Wood and its name celebrates the Silver Jubilee of King George V in 1935. Acquired by the Forestry Commission in 1920, it produces over 40,000 tons of timber a year. Most of the trees are now conifers, however, with very few birch, oak, alder, ash or willow surviving. Polecats, otters and pine martin can be found,

Pistyll Cain

while you stand a good chance of spotting fallow deer. The exotic firs have also given the native red squirrel a haven from the American invader, the grey squirrel. Look for heron in the rivers, famous for salmon and sea trout. A short diversion is made to admire two water-falls, Rhaeadr Mawddach and Pistyll-y-Cain. Another diversion takes you to the Gwynfynyd Gold Mine. Hundreds of men were employed here around 1900 and production peaked at 20,000oz of gold in one year. Closure came in 1914 but a brief revival was experienced in the 1980s. There is still gold here but it is too expensive to extract. You can try your luck (and take home what you find) on a visit to this mine. The mine is open as a tourist attraction all year. Opening hours are from 9am to 7pm between April and October. Telephone 0341 423332 for details of open-ing hours in the winter. There is a courtesy bus from Dolgellau in the summer. Board it at the Welsh Gold Centre in Dolgellau.

The Walk

1. Cross the A470 carefully and bear left down a signposted path to the river. Cross the bridge to the picnic place and go left along a forest track, keeping above the Afon Mawddach on your left.

2. Turn left across the footbridge at junction 51 and bear left up to a lane. Go left along it but bear right when a track forks from it. The track eventually converges with the lane, which you go right along.

3. Fork right uphill until the turning to Cefndeuddwr on your right. Go ahead along the rough track and ignore a downhill path at junction 22. When an inviting forest track forks left downhill, go straight ahead along the higher track,

4. Turn sharply right at junction 23. Go ahead at a crosstracks (junction 24) and pass a waymarked descending path at junction 32. Go down to junction 31 and over a crosstracks to reach the bridge over the Afon Gain.

5. Cross the bridge and bear right with a broad track until it bends left. Go straight ahead along a waymarked forest path (look for a white-topped post and white painted footprints). Go right downhill at junction 30 to reach a bridge over the Afon Mawddach.

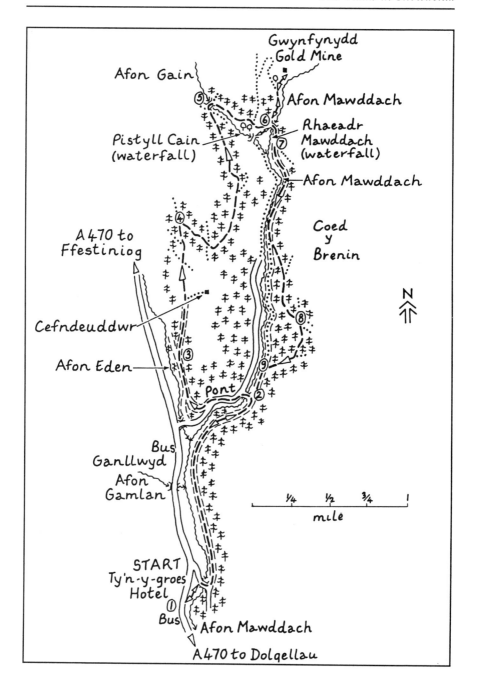

6. Before crossing the bridge (and you will cross it, so you can safely leave your granny on it), divert left along the track which keeps above the river on your right to reach Gwynfynydd Gold Mine. Retrace your steps to the bridge, pass it on your left and continue to see the two waterfalls, Rhaeadr Mawddach on your left and Pistyll Cain (where the track goes ahead over another bridge) on your right. Once again retrace your steps to the bridge over the Afon Mawddach and, at last, cross it. Turn right to follow the firm track which keeps above the river on your right. Climb to junction 19.

7. Go right along the track above the river on your right. Fork left uphill at the next junction (20). Ignore a track descending from your left. Go ahead to pass a viewpoint on your right. Reach a crosstracks at junction 12.

8. Turn right downhill. Ignore a rough track on your left. Descend with power lines, pass junction 11 and walk with a stream on your left.

9. Bear left at junction 10 to follow the valley track above the river on your right again. Pass the footbridge crossed at direction 2 (now on your right) and go ahead to retrace your steps to the Ty'n-y-groes Hotel.

The Ty'n-y-groes Hotel.

18. PENMAENPOOL

Route: George III Hotel, Penmaenpool – Line of Dismantled Railway – Pont Abergwynant – Kings Youth Hostel – Gellilwyd Farm – Maes Angharad – George III Hotel, Penmaenpool.

Distance: 7 miles.

Map: O.S. Outdoor Leisure 23 (Snowdonia – Cadair Idris area).

Start: George III Hotel, Penmaenpool (SH 694185).

Access: Penmaenpool is on the A493 two miles west of Dolgellau. A toll bridge provides a short cut across the Mawddach Estuary for the A496 to Barmouth. Sadly, there is no ferry-boat service, while even the railway halt was made redundant when the line was closed in 1965. At least there is still a bus service (No. 28 from Tywyn and Dolgellau). There is a car park.

George III, Penmaenpool (0341 423565)

The King of Tonga and Roald Dahl are just two of the famous guests who have been enchanted by the view across the Mawddach Estuary to Diffwys. Gerard Manley Hopkins reputedly wrote his poem *Penmaenpool* in an old hotel guest book. It's worth repeating:

Who long for rest, who look for pleasure
Away from counter, court or school
O where live well your lease of leisure
But here at, here at Penmaen Pool?

You'll dare the Alp you'll dart the skiff?
Each sport has here its tackle and tool:
Come, plant the staff of Cadair cliff;
Come, swing the sculls on Penmaen Pool.

What's yonder? – Grizzled Dyphwys dim:
The triple-hummocked Giant's stool,
Hoar messmate, hobs and nobs with him
To halve the bowl of Penmaen Pool.

And all the landscape under survey,
At tranquil turns, by nature's rule,
Rides repeated topsy-turvy
In frank, in fairy Penmaen Pool.

And Charles's Wain, the wondrous seven,
And sheep-flock clouds like worlds of wool,
For all they shine so, high in heaven,
Shew brighter shaken in Penmaen Pool.

The Mawddach, how she trips! though throttled
If floodtime teeming thrills her full,
And mazy sands all water-wattled
Waylay her at ebb, past Penmaen Pool.

But what's to see in stormy weather,
When grey showers gather and gusts are cool?-
Why, raindrop-roundels looped together
That lave the face of Penmaen Pool.

Then even in weariest wintry hour
Of New Year's month or surly Yule
Furred snows, charged tuft above tuft, tower
From darksome darksome Penmaen Pool

And ever, if bound here hardest home,
You've parlour-pastime left and (who'll
Not honour it?) ale like goldy foam
That frocks an oar in Penmaen Pool.

Then come who pine for peace or pleasure
Away from counter, court, or school,
Spend here your measure of time and treasure
And taste the treats of Penmaen Pool.

The main hotel was built in the 17th century and was once two buildings. One was a pub, while the other was a ship chandlers, serving the local boat building industry. They were combined to form a hotel in 1890, the year after Gerard Manley Hopkins died. In 1977, the nearby redundant railway station was turned into a lodge for the hotel, which is also renowned for its food. During the summer months the cellar bar is open to serve a cold buffet, toasted sandwiches and pizzas.

The George III hotel

The Mawddach Estuary

The Mawddach Estuary is one of the most loved in Europe. Bird-watchers flock here to spot many types of duck and wading birds. Visit the RSPB Wildlife Centre in the old railway signal box near the hotel. At least this and the Morfa Mawddach Walk along the old track bed is a little compensation for the loss of one of the most scenic railway journeys in the world. Trains ceased running on this line, which used to form part of the route between Barmouth and Manchester via Ruabon and Dolgellau, in 1965. This was exactly one hundred years since the railway reached here. Before that, the sea was the main thoroughfare. Smuggling went on, while the local oak trees were cut down to build boats. The Brigantine **Geraldine** was built here in 1841.

The Walk

1. Face the estuary and turn left along the line of the dismantled railway. This soon cuts inland away from the estuary on your right. Approach a bridge over a tributary stream (Gwynant).

2. Bear left just before the bridge to descend to cross a small wooden footbridge, as waymarked by a yellow arrow. Walk away from the estuary with the stream (Gwynant) on your right. Follow the waymarked track to pass woodland on your left. Pass a wall on your right, with a ladder stile in it, to reach a waymarked gate. Bear right through this to take the track across a meadow and walk with Gwynant on your right again. Go ahead through a gate near a signpost. Continue down a lane beside the stream on your right, ignoring two bridges across it. Reach the A493 road and go left for 30 yards, then bear right up the access lane to Kings Youth Hostel.

3. The access lane to the youth hostel makes a fine walk through a wooded valley. Pass an outbuilding of the youth hostel on your left, then fork left to pass the main youth hostel building on your right. Continue over a bridge and up the lane ahead. This soon deteriorates into a rough track as it passes through a farmyard (the farm is an independent bunkhouse) and turns right to take the higher gate. Climb with what is an unclassified county road for 60 yards to a junction.

4. The unclassified county road (not marked on the Ordnance Survey Map but a public highway) turns sharply left uphill. It is a road in theory only, being a grassy, rocky track, waymarked by white arrows. Continue beside a tumbled wall on your right. Pass a farm building on your left, then bear left from the obvious track to take the waymarked gate in a wall ahead. Go ahead along a glorious, rough, track, with inspiring views of Cadair Idris over the wall on your right. Maintain this direction when you come to a small, wooden,

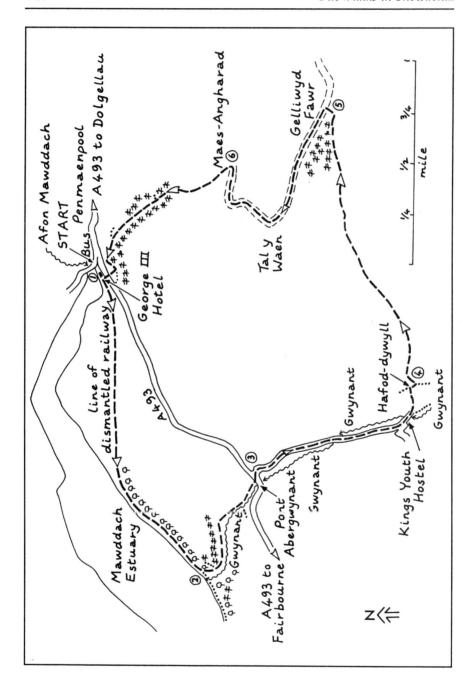

gate. Eventually the walled track ends at a small, metal, gate. Go ahead through this to follow the clear path over open moorland. Approach a walled plantation of conifer trees on your left, go ahead through the metal gate in a fence ahead and descend to a track. Turn left to pass a ruin on your left and follow the track between a fence on your left and a wall on your right. Cross the ladder stile beside a gate ahead to reach a lane.

5. Turn left along the lane (another unclassified county road not shown on the Ordnance Survey map). Pass Gellilwyd Fawr on your right. Reach Tal y Waen, where there is a private farm trail (admission fee payable). Follow the (public) lane as it bends right and pass the access track to Tynllwyn on your left. Continue along the lane as it bends left to go through a gate across it. Walk with a wall on your left and a fence on your right. The lane bends gently left, then sharply right to go ahead through a gate. Approach another gate.

6. Just before the next gate, turn left over a waymarked ladder stile. Cross a field to take another ladder stile in the wall opposite. Continue as waymarked to pass the farmhouse of Maes-Angharad on your right. Go down a muddy track to a waymarked gate before a stream. Go ahead, veering very slightly left over a field to pass trees on your left to reach a waymarked stile in a wall ahead. Go right to pass a cottage on your left and take a waymarked gate (which you are reminded to shut). Follow the grassy track ahead until it bends right. Bear left here, as waymarked, to reach a ladder stile and cross into a forest. Go down a path to a forest track. Bear left along this, immediately passing a pond on your right. Descend gradually to pass above Penmaenpool's toll bridge on your right. Notice a small metal gate in the wall on your right and turn through it, as waymarked. Descend with a woodland path down to the A493 road. Turn right back to the George III Hotel which is soon below on your left.

19. DOLGELLAU

Route: Stag Inn, Dolgellau – Penbrynglas – Trefeilia – Tabor – Dref-gerig – Pant-y-Onnen – Coed Croes – Heol Feurig – Stag Inn, Dolgellau.

Distance: 6 miles.

Map: O.S. Outdoor Leisure 23 (Snowdonia – Cadair Idris area).

Start: The Stag Inn, Dolgellau (SH 728179)

Access: Motorists won't have far to walk from the official, signed, car park at Marian Mawr, Dolgellau, for this pub. Situated in Bridge Street, near Y Bont Fawr over the Afon Wnion, the Stag Inn is also within easy reach of the bus stops in Eldon Square. Dolgellau is the hub for the local bus services in Meirionnydd, including the long distance No. 2 route between Aberystwyth and Caernarfon and the No. 94 from Wrexham.

The Stag Inn, Dolgellau (0341 422533)

One of the oldest inns in Dolgellau, perhaps the oldest, the Stag has featured in Camra's Good Beer Guide since 1978. Food is available here too. There is a beer garden and family room. The opening hours are 11 am to 11 pm on weekdays, 12 noon to 3 pm and 7 pm to 10.30 pm on Sundays

Dolgellau

Dolgellau was a county capital until the creation of Gwynedd in 1974. It may soon resume its former role when the reorganization of Welsh county boundaries should bring back the county of Meirionnydd. It is a stone-built town, full of squares and winding, crooked streets. The impression is of a closely-packed bastion with a female nature, as opposed to, for example, the broad, long and straight male identity of Machynlleth. Welsh language, culture and nationalism have found a secure haven here at the foot of the mighty Cadair Idris. Owain Glyndwr stayed here in 1404 and wrote to Charles VII of France from the town.

Cadair Idris looms over Dolgellau

The woollen industry became the chief concern from the 16th century. Spinning and weaving was done in the cottages, while there were plenty of fulling mills (remembered by the name 'pandy') to treat the cloth before it was sold to merchants. 1657 was a significant year, bringing the visit of George Fox, the Quaker. Local people were attracted by his message that men and women could have direct personal communion with God, obviating the need for outer creeds, rites or church hierarchies. Fox taught them to listen to 'the Inner Light' and follow the word of Jesus in all things. This included refusing to swear an oath of any sort. This led to persecution after the Restoration of Charles II in 1660, when Quakers who refused to take the Oath of Allegiance were deemed to be traitors. Forced to emigrate, William Penn promised the Welsh Quakers their own self-governing and Welsh-speaking territory in Pennsylvania. One emigrant was Rowland Ellis from Bryn-mawr, which is just south of Dolgellau and passed by this walk. He called his new home in America by the same name and it was later given to the famous women's college there.

Sadly, the English-speaking Quakers failed to keep their promise to the Welsh and many disillusioned Welsh Quakers returned home. Their Meeting House was at Tabor, east of Dolgellau. It is still a place of worship today, but for Congregationalists. Dolgellau now has a Quaker Heritage Centre above Ty Meirion, the Snowdonia National Park Visitor Centre in Eldon Square. The fine meadowland behind the Stag Inn and beyond the car park is the home of one of the oldest cricket clubs in Wales. This area was once covered by the sea, from which it derives its name, the Marian. St. Mary's Church has unique wooden pillars. These are tree trunks which were hewn octagonally at the bottom and cylindrically higher up. Oxen were teamed to drag them over the pass from the forest of Mawddwy.

The Walk

1. With your back to the Stag Inn, go right (away from the bridge). Fork left to Queens Square, where Llys Owain (Owain's Palace) reminds you of Glyndwr's connection with Dolgellau. Go ahead to Eldon Square. Turn left in the far corner to enter Smithfield Square and go ahead along Arran Road. Cross the road bridge over the Afon Arran.

2. Turn right immediately after crossing the bridge. Pass houses on your left and walk upstream with the river on your right. Continue up an estate road (Penbrynglas) with Cadair Idris looming ahead. Take the right hand fork at the tannery. Follow a track, which climbs steeply. It levels out and bears left to provide fine views of Cadair Idris on your right. Emerge on a lane and go left along it, walking upstream beside a stream on your right, for 100 yards. When the lane bends left, look for a signposted bridleway on your right.

3. Turn right up the signposted bridleway. Walk upstream with the stream on your right and a fence on your left. Go ahead through a gate and over a cattle grid. Pass Trefeilia on your left, step across a brook to take the gate ahead and continue for 20 yards to a junction of muddy tracks. Bear left uphill, through woodland. When the track approaches a wall and bends right, go left to take a small metal gate near the corner. Continue with a wall on your left and trees on your right. Go through a small metal gate in a fence ahead. The wall soon bears left.

4. When the wall bears left, look for a path which bears right uphill. This turns right and continues through a gap in the upper wall. Go ahead parallel to a wall on your left. Continue through a gate in a corner to walk past a gate on your right and beside a wall on your right. Reach a cottage on your right (this is Pen-yr-allt). Turn left to pass a ruin on your left and go ahead through a gap in the wall. Cross the field to take another gap and walk with a wall on your right. Go ahead through a gate and beside a fence on your right. Turn right through a gate just before the next corner and turn left immediately to walk with a wall topped by a fence on your left. Bear left when the wall ends and go through a gate to turn right along a fenced track. Follow this through a gate ahead and past buildings. Continue through another gate to reach a house on your right. Bear left with the track down to a minor road at a signpost. Turn right up the road. Pass a telephone box on your left and reach the old Quaker Meeting House on the corner with a road on your left. This has been a Congregational Chapel since 1847 and the Quaker graveyard is not here but down the road to the north of Tyddyn Garreg.

5. Continue past the present chapel and former Meeting House on your left. Turn right up a lane and cross a stile beside a gate. Follow a

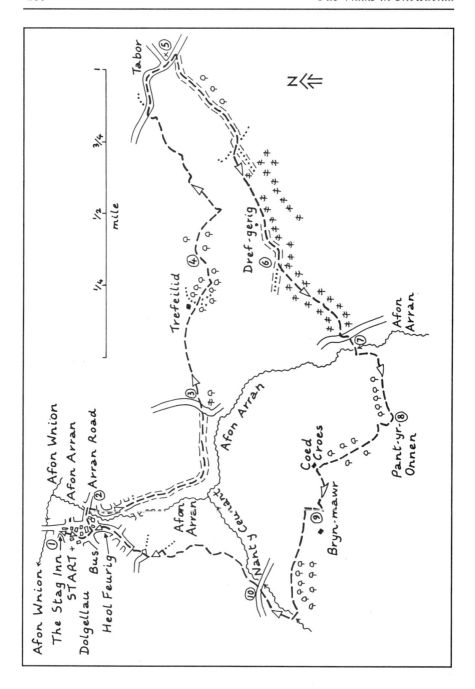

rough but firm track (an unclassified county road). Eventually this veers slightly left to a gate into a forest. The unclassified county road departs from the track about 125 yards before this forest gate, at the point where a wall on your right turns right. Bear right, away from the track, to accompany the wall for 10 yards, then fork left along a grassy path which leads down to a metal gate in the wall about 25 yards lower than the wooden gate taken by the track into the forest. Go ahead through this lower, metal, gate to follow a walled track running parallel to the firm track on your left. Descend to follow a wall on your right and pass trees on your left. Pass Dref-Gerig on your right. Continue along a firmer track which descends to cross a stream. The track then bears right through a forest.

6. About 100 yards along the forest track beyond the stream, fork left to follow a signposted forest path. Ford a stream and emerge on a road beside a signpost and to the right of a bungalow. Turn left along the road for 20 yards.

7. Recent diversions to the public path network from now on may not appear on your Ordnance Survey map for a while, so pay close attention to these notes. Turn right off the road to take a gate and follow the signposted path along the access track to Pandy Gader. Please remember to shut the gates as you pass Pandy Gader on your left, then bear right to cross a footbridge over the Afon Arran. Turn left along a walled track. Pass a ruin on your right and follow a wall on your right to the top corner. Turn right with the track here. Go ahead through a gate to pass Hafodygoeswen on your left. The right of way goes over a wall topped by a fence, but there is a small metal gate in it to the left of the right of way. Having reached the other side of Hafodygoeswen's wall, walk with another wall on your right for 15 yards, then turn right through a small metal gate. Cross a small field. Reach a stone step stile in the wall on your left in the top right corner. Go over it and turn right to follow the wall on your right (ignoring a metal gate in it soon after the stone stile). After about 150 yards, turn right through a gap in the wall and turn left through woodland. Take a gap in the wall ahead and pass above Pant-yr-Onnen on your right.

8. Turn right down the track just after Pant-yr-Onnen. Pass outbuildings and turn left, initially with a wall on your left. Cross a drainage ditch,

pass a spring beneath a tree and bear right to a metal gate in a fence near its corner with a wall. Go through this and over a subsequent stream. Bear right and join a track coming from your left. Continue through a gap in a wall and reach a farm building. Descend with a track and turn left at a junction to pass the new house of Coed Croes on your right and old buildings on your left. Ford a stream, follow the waymarked and recently diverted path ahead, keeping the fence on your right. Cross a ladder stile in the fence ahead. Follow a broken wall topped by a fence on your right and cross a footbridge over a stream. Go through a small metal gate to turn right, as waymarked, in the next field. Descend with a stream on your right to a track near a farm building. This track comes from Bryn-mawr (the home of Rowland Ellis, the Quaker) uphill on your left. Do not go left up this private track.

9. Follow the track down past a farm building and turn left to cross a field, walking parallel to a wall on your left. Go ahead through a gap in the wall facing you. Pass a ruin on your left and a building which has retained its roof. Go ahead over a stream and through a gap in the next corner. Keep beside a wall on your left. Go ahead in the next corner and walk with the wall on your left. As you approach a stream and are level with a ruin which has a tree growing in it on your right, turn left through a gap in the wall. Turn right immediately, as waymarked. Reach a stream, which has to be forded. Turn right downstream and reach a roadside signpost.

10. Cross the road and take the gate facing you. Follow the path which reveals views of the Rhinogydd as you descend to a gate in a wall on your left. Take the enclosed path to Dolgellau. Pass a signposted stile on your right. Turn right down a track at another signpost. Bear left down to the town, passing the Post Office on your right in Heol Feurig. This leads to Eldon Square, where you go ahead to retrace your steps to the Stag Inn.

20. ARAN FAWDDWY

Route: Red Lion Inn, Dinas Mawddwy – Blaencywarch – Aran Fawddwy – Drws Bach – Hengwm – Aber-cywarch – Red Lion Inn, Dinas Mawddwy.

Distance: 14 miles

Map: O.S. Outdoor Leisure 23 (Snowdonia – Cadair Idris area).

Start: The Red Lion Inn (Gwesty'r Llew Coch), Dinas Mawddwy (SH 859148).

Access: Dinas Mawddwy lies below the A470 about 10 miles east of Dolgellau. The Red Lion is on one corner of a road junction at the northern end of the village. There are parking spaces for cars, but this is a long day's walk, so it might be better to park in Y Plas. Buses run to Dinas Mawddwy from Machynlleth (No. S18), where there is the nearest railway station, and from Dolgellau (No. 27). Currently, it's only Wednesdays and Saturdays from Machynlleth and summer Thursdays plus Tuesdays and Fridays all year from Dolgellau. Telephone 0286 679378 for the latest timetable information.

Gwesty'r Llew Coch/Red Lion Inn, Dinas Mawddwy (0650 531247)

You won't find many pubs older than this one. Dating from at least the 12th century, it exudes character. Henry I's illegitimate son by Nest, the Duke of Gloucester, is said to have supped here. Perhaps this was when his mother passed through the place in the arms of Owain, Prince of Powys and son of Cadwgan, son of Bleddyn, in 1107. Most visitors were drovers and they used to shoe their cattle behind the old building, where the toilets are now (there is a modern extension, while the main building was rebuilt as recently as the 16th century). The rear car park was where markets were held, while the farmers met and ate upstairs. Amazingly, the pub doesn't have a resident ghost, but the public toilets just across the road are haunted by a silver-haired man. Film-makers are attracted to this pub, staying here in the early days of colour television to make a children's serial about the supernatural, called 'The Owl Service', which was set in this area. A television documentary has also contrasted a day in the life of Dinas Mawddwy with that of Liverpool. In 1974, Prince Philip was to dine here to mark the opening of an equipped Mountain Rescue Hut at Bryn Hafod (Blaencywarch), but he was replaced at the last minute by Sir John Hunt, of Everest fame. You can dine and stay the night here too. Real ale is served, including Worthington Dark, while the opening hours are 11 am to 11 pm on weekdays, 12 noon to 3 pm and 7 pm to 10.30 pm on Sundays.

The Red Lion Inn

Aran Fawddwy

Even pub walkers are expected to climb a mountain in Snowdonia. The fact that Aran Fawddwy, at 2971 ft, is the highest peak in Britain south of the Snowdon range comes as a surprise to many. Unlike its Meirion-nydd neighbour, the 2928 ft Cadair Idris, it is a shy, secretive, mountain. This conforms with the belief that Mawddwy (of which Fawddwy is a mutation – pronounce it 'Mouthwee') means the territory of the goddess, Mawdd. This is a feminine mountain, whereas Cadair Idris is clearly the seat of a male giant.

Treat this rugged peak with respect, especially in winter. Don't attempt these 14 miles unless you can start early and take all day. Even then, carry a torch and batteries in case you finish after sunset. Make no mistake, this is a strenuous mountain walk to be undertaken only in good weather. Telephone 0898 505285 for a weather forecast and prepare for the worst even if it's fine. Good walking boots are essential, while a windproof and waterproof coat, spare pullover and an adequate supply of food and drink should be carried in a rucksack. Lots of emergency snack bars are best, while a chill wind can demand gloves and hat on the sunniest of days. Whatever you do, don't bring a dog. Much of this route follows courtesy paths where the landowners require that no dogs must be allowed. Take a dog here and, apart from the danger of it being shot by the farmer, you risk ruining years of delicate negotiations and depriving others of access to the Arans in the future.

Another bone of contention is the use of the head of the common in Cwm Cywarch for unofficial car parking and toilets. An official car park has been proposed, but is this most attractive of valleys to be spoilt with a car park? Isn't the answer to encourage 'the long walk in' and make Dinas Mawddwy, with its Red Lion Inn, your base? This should also give walkers an opportunity to contribute to the local economy, instead of just driving in and out from England. Farm incomes in Meirionnydd are declining and this is a blow to the Welsh Language and culture. With their backs to the wall, the local Welsh farmers go against the traditional Welsh freedom to roam over mountain pasture and have fought to deny access. A few courtesy paths (not rights of way) have been agreed and the farmers have received money. There is a danger of this creating a precedent and future access to such places being for rich permit-holders only. No doubt you'll find a local farmer who'll drive this point home over a pint in the Red Lion.

The author at the summit of Aran Fawddwy (2971')

Leave the valley at Blaencywarch, near Bryn Hafod. This Mountain Club hut was opened in 1965. It stands near an old lead mine which was worked in the 18th century. Some machinery dating from the 19th century lies near the hut, but lead was mined here as long ago as Roman times. The steep climb brings you to a ravine where a farmer once dropped a pot of salted butter which he was taking to market. The ruin of an old hafod, or summer dwelling for shepherds, can be seen. Sheep graze on the lush grass now, but cattle used to be kept up here. A bull once chased a man to seek refuge on top of a prominent standing stone. Not far away, a circular compound was built to catch foxes.

Turning right to walk along the spine of the Arans, you pass Tyllau Mwn, the mine shafts of Friar's Coat mine. When the intrepid Elizabeth Baker came here in October, 1770, she was caught in hail and 'the rain ran off (her) petticoats as they were too wet to receive more'. She came in search of copper but suspected iron and silver – the metals that 'constitute what is called the Friars Coat'.

As you approach the summit, you pass the site of an aircrash on your right. A De Havilland Mark 9 Photo-Reconnaissance Mosquito met its end on 9th February, 1944, whilst on a cross-country exercise. Attached to 540 Squadron, it came from RAF Benson, in Oxfordshire. It had carried out 16 successful sorties over enemy territory between June, 1943, and January, 1944, covering Turin, Milan, Nuremburg, Munich, Berlin, Paris and Toulouse, but the crew of two, including a Polish pilot, were both killed here. Their bodies weren't found until 14th February. Closer to the summit, a Republic P47 Thunderbolt crashed on 16th September, 1944, with the pilot losing his life.

The view from the summit is well worth the effort of the climb. Cadair Idris, the Rhinogs, Snowdon, Arenig Fawr, Bala Lake, the Berwyns and Pumlumon can all be seen. The summit cairn was built by the men of Mawddwy when they heard a (false) rumour that Cadair Idris was higher than their beloved Aran (high place). Two more aircraft have crashed near it. A Bristol Beaufighter was lost in cloud on 10th February, 1945 (a year and a day after the De Havilland Mark 9). Both crew members, including an Australian pilot, were killed. The plane had flown from RAF Pershore. On 17th May, 1945, an American P-51 Mustang dived out of formation to crash here, killing the pilot.

A fine view of the peak overlooking Creiglyn Dyfi, the source of the Afon Dyfi, can be had on the descending path at Drws Bach (little door). Take care here, especially in mist, and pause at the memorial to SAC Mike Aspain of RAF St. Athan mountain rescue team. He was killed by lightning near here whilst on duty on 5th June, 1960. Open the heavy box at the base of the cairn to sign the book and leave a few coins for charity (including the RAF Benevolent Fund).

The Walk

(Don't underestimate how long and strenuous this mountain walk is)

1. With your back to the Red Lion Inn, turn right to face the public toilets and turn right again down the minor road to Bwlch y Groes, where the highest public road in Wales (reaching 1790 ft) forks to Bala Lake on the left and Lake Vyrnwy on the right. Cross a bridge over the Afon Cerist, a tributary of the Afon Dyfi, and go left along the signposted public footpath (but not along the track to the caravan site below it). Take a gate ahead and continue to climb gradually with a hedge on your right. Pass through a patch of woodland and climb to a gate in the top fence.

2. Go through the gate to join an old cart road and turn right along it. This leads to a junction where you bear left up the No Through Road and ignore the road (to Bwlch y Groes) on your right. Follow this road to its end, then maintain your direction along a muddy track to join a road near where it crosses the Afon Cywarch by a bridge.

3. Go left along the road up Cwm Cywarch. Pass a signposted path to the Arans which crosses a footbridge on your right. Continue through a gate across the road to walk near the river on your right. Ignore the access drive to Blaencywarch farmhouse ahead. Fork right, as signposted. Notice a footbridge over the river on your right and go left for 20 yards, then turn right to follow a wall on your left. Go ahead over two ladder stiles beside gates. Leave the track 200 yards before Bryn Hafod. Turn left with the wall, as waymarked.

4. Cross a stile to the right of a gate. Go ahead, then turn right to follow the waymarked path up the valley. This crosses the stream by a

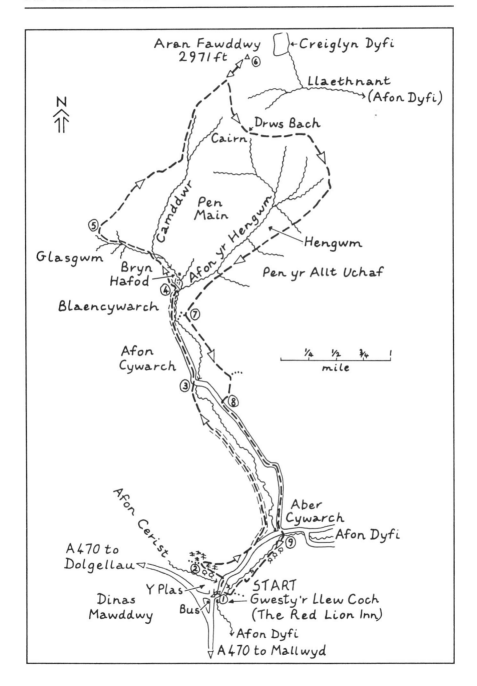

Aran Fawddwy
2971ft △⑥ ◁─Creiglyn Dyfi

N ⇑

Llaethnant
→(Afon Dyfi)

Drws Bach

Cairn

Camddwr

Pen
Main

Afon yr Hengwm

Hengwm

⑤

Glasgwm

Bryn
Hafod

④

Pen yr Allt Uchaf

Blaencywarch

⑦

Afon
Cywarch

¼ ½ ¾ 1
mile

③

⑧

Afon Cerist

Aber
Cywarch

A470 to
Dolgellau ▽

Afon Dyfi

②

⑨

Y Plas

START

Dinas
Mawddwy

Bus ▽

①─ Gwesty'r Llew Coch
(The Red Lion Inn)

↓Afon Dyfi

▽A470 to Mallwyd

footbridge. Climb to pass a fence on your left and pass a ruined hafod.

5. Turn right to follow the waymarked path, pass a peaty pond on your left. Continue beside a fence on your left and ignore a ladder stile in it. Boards help you over boggy places. Cross a stile in a corner ahead and keep beside the fence on your left. Don't cross the stile in the next corner. Go right to keep the fence on your left, soon turning left with it. Ignore another stile in it. Continue with the fence on your left and eventually reach a top corner where you go ahead over a stile. Turn left to cross another stile and turn right immediately to go along the rocky ridge to the summit of Aran Fawddwy.

6. Retrace your steps to the stile in the fence. Turn left across it. Ignore the stile on your right. Descend with the fence on you right to a lower stile. Cross this to walk with the fence now on your left. Pass the memorial cairn and sign the book at Drws Bach. Follow the path when it veers right away from the fence. Cross a stile in a fence ahead and keep descending with a fence on your left. When this bears left at a boggy plateau, go right to a waymark post. Follow the good path which descends gradually along the southern side of Hengwm. The track in the valley bottom is private! Go ahead over two stiles then, when the path is much lower and wider, cross a stile beside a gate to continue down a fenced track. Fork right, as waymarked, to take an enclosed path.

7. Turn left over a signposted stile beside a gate. Pass a ruin on your left and go ahead over another stile beside a gate to walk past trees on your left and past a farm building. Continue over a stile beside a gate to pass farm buildings on your left and veer right across an access track to walk beside a fence on your left. Veer left to cross another stile and turn right immediately to cross the bottom of a field and take the stile above a gate in the next corner. Go ahead to cross a stream by a footbridge and pass an old farm building shaded by trees. The right of way veers slightly left to cross a stile, continue over another stile and across a field to Ceunant. Ignore the path going over a stile on your left, but turn right over the bridge and follow the track down to the road in Cwm Cywarch.

8. Go left along the road to join the Bwlch y Groes road at Aber-

cywarch. Bear left across this to turn right down the public footpath to a footbridge across the Afon Dyfi.

9. After crossing the footbridge, turn right to walk with the river on your right, going downstream. There is a new diversion here which will take time to appear on the Ordnance Survey maps. Basically, follow the river until forced up above the trees. Look for steps in the corner ahead and turn right down these back to the river. Turn left to continue beside the river on your right back to another footbridge. Cross this, on your right, to go ahead over the common to the road. Turn left to climb with the road back to the Red Lion Inn, Dinas Mawddwy, on your left.

21. LLWYNGWRIL

Route: Garthangharad Inn, Llwyngwril – Standing Stones – Ffordd Ddu – Garthangharad Inn, Llwyngwril

Distance: 9 miles

Map: O.S. Outdoor Leisure 23 (Snowdonia – Cadair Idris area)

Start: The Garthangharad Inn, Llwyngwril (SH 592096)

Access: Llwyngwril is on the A493 road between Tywyn and Fairbourne. There is a railway station on the Cambrian Coast Line (Machynlleth – Pwllheli) on the western edge of the village, while the No 28 bus between Tywyn and Dolgellau stops near the school, across the bridge from the Garthangharad Inn, which is in the centre of the village.

The Garthangharad Inn, Llwyngwril (0341 250484)

The outgoing landlord and landlady regaled me with vivid tales of the resident poltergeist. Watch out for flying glasses. Part of the building, which dates from 1736, used to be a mortuary. It was a pub when the first world war broke out and has become a favourite of Worcestershire cricketers. Ken Byers, who played for the county, was a previous landlord and Basil D'Oliveira liked to visit the place. Real ale is served and food is available, including vegetarian fare. The opening hours are noon to 3pm and 7pm to 11pm on weekdays, noon to 3pm and 7pm to 10.30pm on Sundays.

Ancient Trackways

It is a curious fact that the western fringe of Great Britain is littered with ancient monuments. Did the people who erected them travel by sea from the west? Was there an Atlantis? Enough of such speculation. Enjoy the company of prehistoric standing stones as you follow a track which was, presumably, used by the people who erected the stones, north of Llwyngwril. As you reach the plateau, the sky seems to come closer and the modern world slips away, out of sight. It is easy to imagine yourself back into the days of *The Mabinogion*, the great collection of ancient Welsh stories. The birds of Rhiannon seem to fly above you and a hint of mist suggests that the goddess herself may appear from it. Of course, the view we enjoy overlooking Cardigan Bay was probably very different when the standing stones were being erected. There may well have been a fertile coastal plain, flooded by the sea within our ancestral memory and known as Cantre'r Gwaelod (see the Aberdyfi walk). Return along the Ffordd Ddu (the Black Road), a prehistoric route linking the Dysynni Valley at Llanegryn with the standing stones around the Llynnau Cregennen above the Mawddach estuary.

The old millstone at Felin Uchaf, Llwyngwril

The Walk

1. With your back to the Garthangharad Inn, go left up Ffordd y Coleg and follow the No Through Road with the Afon Gwril on your right. Soon bear left, away from it and ignoring a track which forks right. Climb with the lane to overlook Cardigan bay on your left.

2. Go through a gate across the lane and keep climbing with it. Ignore farm tracks on both sides. The land's surface deteriorates and you pass a signposted public footpath descending on your left. Take a second gate across the lane. When the lane bears right through a gate towards Parth-y-gwyddwch, go straight ahead up the grassy track which is initially lined by stone walls. Continue beside a fence on your right and go through a wooden gate ahead.

3. Take the metal gate in the next corner and follow the track as it bears right around open hillside. Pass a ruin on your left, then go through a waymarked gate in a stone wall ahead. Ignore a turning down to a farm on your left and proceed along what is a metalled lane again. Cross a concrete bridge over the Afon Caletwr. Notice three standing stones, in line, in a field on your left. Keep to the metalled láne, ignoring an inviting downhill track on your left. Admire the view above Fairbourne and across the Mawddach estuary to Barmouth.

4. Go ahead through a gate across the lane which is flanked by a standing stone on your left. A plantation of conifer trees commences on your right and is soon matched by a similar forest on your left.

5. Reach a signposted junction and turn sharply right up a path between the trees. This broad path eventually bears left to a stile in a fence. Cross this to set foot on the prehistoric track known as the Ffordd Ddu.

6. Turn right along the Ffordd Ddu. Keep to this hard track and ignore a grassy track which forks left. Reach a corner, go through a gate across the Ffordd Ddu and turn right with it as it keeps above the Afon Dyffryn on your right. Pay close attention to the hillside on your left. After half a mile, when you reach a fence coming down it to a sheep-fold just beyond a gate in the fence on your left, go ahead along the Ffordd Ddu for 250 yards.

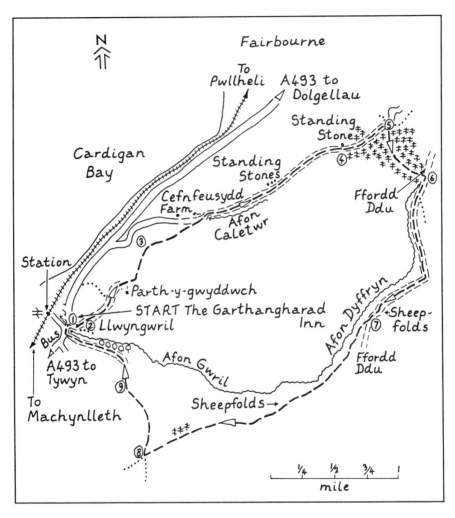

7. Fork right, off the Ffordd Ddu, down a grassy track. This fork starts near where there is another gate in the fence on your left. Keep close to the Afon Dyffryn on your right. Follow the track through a sheep-fold and continue beside a wall on your right. Turn right with the wall, which is replaced by a fence. Continue through a gate ahead and past a plantation of trees on your right.

8. Reach open moorland crossed by power lines. Take the last gate on

your right just before the fence turns right to make a corner. Bear slightly right across this field to go under the power lines and take a gate in the far wall ahead. Continue towards the sea by taking a gate in the next fence. Bear slightly left down to a gap in the wall near the bottom corner ahead.

9. Bear slightly right down the next field to where a grassy track leaves from its bottom corner. Follow this towards the sea, above the wooded valley of the Afon Gwril on your right. Join a rough farm track and bear left with it down to Llwyngwril. Back on the A494 in the village, turn right along the pavement and across the bridge to return to the Garthangharad Inn, on your right.

The Garthangharad Inn

22. MARY JONES' COTTAGE

Route: Railway Inn, Abergynolwyn – Castell y Bere – Mary Jones's Cottage – Pen-y-meint – Pont Ystumanner – Railway Inn, Abergynolwyn.

Distance: 6 miles

Map: O.S. Outdoor Leisure 23 (Snowdonia – Cadair Idris area)

Start: The Railway Inn, Abergynolwyn (SH 678069)

Access: Aberygnolwyn is on the B4405 between Bryncrug and Minffordd. Cars can be parked outside the pub or in the car park across the road. Buses stop at the pub. No. 30 goes between Dolgellau and Tywyn and No. 59 runs between Tywyn and Machynlleth. There is only one proper way to travel here, however. Take the Talyllyn Railway from Tywyn to Abergynolwyn or Nant Gwernol and walk the short distance into the village. Services are seasonal. Telephone 0654 710472 for timetable information.

The Railway Inn, Abergynolwyn (0654 782279)

Despite its name, this has been a pub since at least the 16th century, when it was known as 'Troed Oen' (Lamb's Foot). Definitely a pub for real ale, while the food's alright as well. Opening hours are 11 am to 11 pm on weekdays, 12 noon to 3 pm and 7 pm to 10.30 pm on Sundays. 'The Railway' refers, of course, to the Talyllyn Railway. Ramblers are given a very positive welcome here.

Mary Jones' Cottage

This walk take you down the Dysynni Valley from the old slate village of Abergynolwyn to the side valley formed by the Afon Cadair. Stirring events have taken place here, with Castell y Bere passed by this route. It is the story of an inspired young Welsh girl who lived further up the valley that is best remembered. Here is the very opposite of Tal-y-llyn's feminine charms. Rugged heroism stands all around you. The castle is reached first and must be visited (for free). Unlike Caernarfon or Harlech, this castle was Welsh. It was probably built by Llywelyn-ap-Iorwerth (the Great) about 1221. It stood on a rocky outcrop, where its ruins are now shaded by trees. The valley used to be an estuary and the ground around the castle may have been marshy. Craig yr Aderyn (Bird Rock) was used as a look-out post to warn the Welsh defenders of the approach of any English fleet. Edward I had determined to subjugate Wales and his soldiers killed Prince Llywelyn (the Last) at Builth in 1282. Llywelyn's brother, David, then claimed the title of Prince of Wales. He made Castell-y-Bere (Castle of the Bird of Prey) his base and came under siege here in April, 1283. The castle fell within the month and David was soon betrayed whilst in hiding. He was hanged, drawn and quartered by Edward in Shrewsbury.

The conquerors attempted to develop a town near the castle but were discouraged by an uprising led by Madog in 1294, timed to coincide with Edward's planned invasion of France. Excavations have revealed burnt timber which may date from this period. William Watkin Edward Wynne, of nearby Peniarth, excavated the ruins in the mid 19th century. Some of the finds dated back to Neolithic times, prompting thoughts of a much earlier settlement here (on a clearly visible ley from Devil's Rock through St. Michael's Church and extended to Craig yr Aderyn?).

Whole books have been written about Mary Jones and her Bible. When 16 years old, she walked barefooted for nearly 30 miles over the mountains to Bala. She had saved up to buy a Welsh Bible and heard that the Rev. Thomas Charles had some for sale in that town. She arrived to find they had all been sold, however. When he heard Mary's story, the Rev. Thomas Charles gave her his last, personal, copy and was inspired to go on to found the British and Foreign Bible Society four years later, in 1804. This organisation remembered what had caused its formation. The story of Mary Jones' walk was published for world-wide distribution in 1882, 18 years after its heroine had been buried in the graveyard of the chapel at her married home of Bryncrug, after living to be 80. This walk leads to Tyn-y-ddôl, where the ruins of the cottage that Mary set out from in 1800 can be seen. A plaque records her story.

Castell y Bere

The Walk

1. Go left from the Railway Inn and turn left immediately. Follow the road towards Llanegryn, crossing a bridge over the Afon Dysynni and climbing to a junction with a minor road on your right. Go ahead, keeping above the Afon Dysynni on your left.

2. Reach a stile and a signpost on your right. Bear right over the stile to follow this path over the shoulder of Foel Cae'rberllan. Approach some oak trees and reach a slate stile in the wall on your right, near a corner. Cross the stile, go down steps and cross a stream to continue with the wall on your left. Take a gate in the corner and descend to a track below.

3. Go right along this track. Turn left through a metal kissing-gate and turn half-right to cross the field diagonally to a stile beside a signpost in the bottom right hand corner. This gives access to a road. Turn right along this road and pass Castell y Bere on your left. Continue past Llanfihangel-y-pennant's church dedicated to St. Michael. This route links with the Tal-y-llyn walk here. Follow the road to Tyn-y-ddol, on the far side of the Afon Cadair. The ruins of Mary Jones' Cottage are on your right.

4. Turn left through a gate and follow the path which accompanies the Afon Cadair, on your left, downstream. Do not turn left when you reach a bridge over this young river. Go ahead over two ladder stiles and walk with a wall on your left. Emerge over a stile beside a chapel.

5. Go left down a lane. Reach a slightly staggered crossroads near a telephone box. Turn right to follow a road over the Afon Dysynni at Pont Ystumanner.

6. Turn left through a gate to follow the signposted path up the Dysynni Gorge. Keep the river on your left.

7. Bear left at a building to cross a footbridge over the stream, Nant Gwernol. Take a path on your right to the main road and go left back to the Railway Inn, Abergynolwyn.

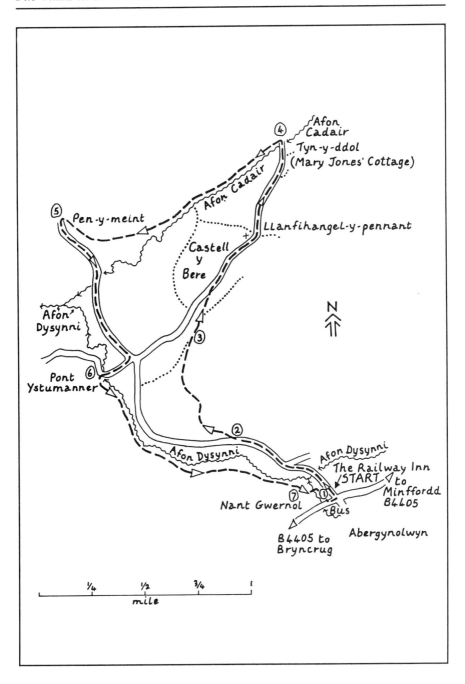

23. TAL-Y-LLYN

Route: Tynycornel Hotel, Tal-y-llyn – Pen-y-Bont Hotel, Tal-y-llyn – Llanfihangel-y-pennant – Pencoed – Devil's Rock – Rhiwogof – Tynycornel Hotel, Tal-y-llyn.

Distance: 9 $1/2$ miles.

Map: O.S. Outdoor leisure 23 (Snowdonia – Cadair Idris area).

Start: Tynycornel Hotel, Tal-y-llyn (SH 714094)

Access: Tyncornel Hotel is on the B4405 about two miles west of its junction with the A487 at Minffordd. Cars can be parked here. Several buses pass the hotel at infrequent intervals. Bus No. 30 runs between Dolgellau and Tywyn, while No. 59 connects Tywyn with Machynlleth via Corris.

The Tynycornel Hotel, Tal-y-llyn (0654 782282)

This Inn was built in 1844 by Colonel Vaughan, of Hengwrt, then the proprietor of the lake upon which it faces. It was to provide comfortable accommodation for anglers. The proper name for Tal-y-Llyn Lake is Llyn Mwyngil. This can be translated as 'lake of the charming retreat'. Its pleasant, relaxing, feminine nature attracted royalty in the early 20th century. Luxury accommodation and exquisite food are still available here, while the bar is open from 11 am to 11 pm on weekdays, 12 noon to 3 pm and 7 pm to 10.30 pm on Sundays.

The Pen-y-bont Hotel, Tal-y-llyn (0654 782285)

This Inn dates back to the 16th century and can boast the ghost of Barlow and his dog, a former resident. Food and accommodation are available here too, while the bar is open from 11 am to 3 pm and 6 pm to 11 pm on weekdays, 12 noon to 3 pm and 7 pm to 10.30 pm on Sundays.

Waterfall, Nant yr Eira

Michael and Mary

The gentle feminine nature of Tal-y-llyn is confirmed by its church being dedicated to St. Mary. Parts of the building date from the 13th century. No nails were used to fix the roof timbers – just wooden pegs. The roof was most probably originally thatched. A striking feature is the tester, or arch, with painted roses. These were probably done in celebration of the end of the Wars of the Roses when Henry Tudor became King in 1485. A translation of the words above the porch are a caution: 'A great holy dwelling place, All hallowed in the presence of God and the multitude, Let no man come hither, But with good thoughts'. Outside is a famous grave. Enter by the lych gate opposite Pen-y-bont Hotel and turn right immediately to see an ornamental cross. This marks the grave of Jenny Jones. Born in Scotland in June, 1789, she spent three days on the field of the Battle of Waterloo. Her husband fought with the 23rd Royal Welch Fusiliers. She died in Tal-y-llyn on 11th April, 1884. This walk leads to the neighbouring parish of Llanfihangel-y-pennant. There is another ancient church here, dedicated to St. Michael. This may be of some significance. Hamish Miller the dowser and co-author, with Paul Broadhurst, of *The Sun and the Serpent* has discovered wandering energy lines which aim for churches dedicated to St. Michael (for male energy) and St. Mary (for female energy). Almost equidistant between the Michael and Mary churches and near the old parish boundary at approximately grid reference SH 690104, lies the Devil's Rock.

This is a large flat stone, now partly buried. In the past people from both parishes would meet here to dance, especially on Easter Sunday. One Easter the devil came in the form of an ass. He let out an unearthly howl that made the mountains tremble. The people fled to their respective parish churches in terror. The two local shepherds, from Pencoed and from Rhiwogof, were later asked to inspect the rock. They discovered the devil had left his hoofprint. They also started the practice of carving their initials and the date into the rock. The oldest date is, reputedly, 1564. This story suggests that this stone was visited for fertility rituals until the Protestants discouraged such practices. If there are male and female energy lines, this would be a good place for them to cross!

The Walk

1. Go left from Tynycornel Hotel to walk with the lake on your right. Reach St. Mary's Church, Tal-y-llyn, on your left. Turn right to pass Pen-y-bont Hotel on your left. Follow the lane with Tal-y-llyn Lake on your right. Approach 'Yr Hen Reithordy' (the Old Rectory).

2. Turn left along the signposted bridleway which goes through the gate before 'Yr Hen Reithordy'. Walk with a wall on your left and a tree-clad steep hillside on your right. Go right at a fork uphill, through the trees. Turn sharply right along a path which climbs to a forest track above the trees. Go left down this to a hairpin bend.

3. Go ahead along another track which ascends gradually. Continue through a gate and above oak trees on your left. Pass a waymarked path descending on your left. Follow the track as it climbs and bends right to a gate and a ladder stile. Cross the stile and walk with a wall on your right. As this bears right and peters out, go left down the valley, putting the stream on your left. Climb a ladder stile beside the next gate, pass a ruined cottage on your right and ford another stream near a second ruined cottage. Walk with the stream, Nant yr Eira, on your left. Go ahead along a track and through a gate, but fork left off the track (which climbs to the right) after 35 yards. Follow a grassy path above the stream on your left. Pass a stile in a fence near a waterfall on your left. Bear right, away from the stream. Cross a stile in the fence on your left and descend to the woodland path which passes waterfalls on your left. Go ahead over a ladder stile beside a gate next to a building. Emerge opposite St. Michael's Church, Llanfihangel-y-pennant.

4. Turn right along the hedged road. Reach a ladder stile beside a gate on your right. Cross it to follow a track which passes above a farm on your left. Eventually cross a flat wooden bridge over a stream (Nant Pencoed). Take the gate ahead and zigzag uphill with the track. Fork right at the top to a sheep-fold and a building (Pencoed).

5. Take a gate on your left and immediately turn right to bear left uphill. Cross a stile near a small wooden gate in the top wall. Turn right to follow the wall on your right. When the wall becomes a

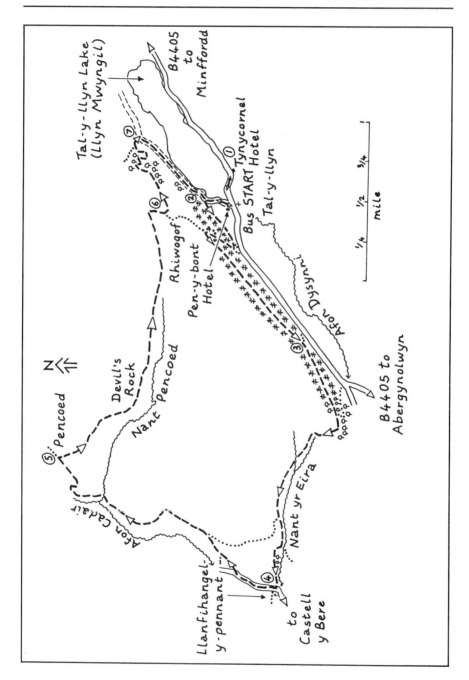

fence, bear right over a stile in it and descend to a ladder stile in a fence running across the valley. Cross this to walk up the valley, keeping well above the stream (Nant Pencoed) on your right. Look for Devil's Rock below a rockface to the left of the path about 125 yards above the wall at a point about 250 yards from where the wall turns across the valley. Continue past a sheep-fold and go up the valley. Join a track coming from your left at its top. Descend with this track towards Rhiwogof, crossing the ladder stiles placed beside the gates across it.

6. Just before Rhiwogof farm, take the ladder stile to the left of a gate and turn left to walk beside a fence on your left. Continue through a waymarked gate and follow the track which passes above trees then descends. Turn right as waymarked by a yellow arrow on a tree above a wooded ravine. Descend to where a waymarked path turns sharply left and follow it across a footbridge. Pass a house on your right and go down to a lane.

7. Go right to follow the lane back to Tal-y-llyn, walking with the lake on your left.

24. CADAIR IDRIS

Route: Minffordd Hotel – Cwm Cau – Craig Cau – Penygadair – Craig Cau – Cwm Cau – Minffordd Hotel

Distance: 6 miles

Map: O.S. Outdoor Leisure 23 (Snowdonia – Cadair Idris area)

Start: Minffordd Hotel (SH 733116)

Access: Minffordd Hotel is beside the A487 between Machynlleth and Dolgellau, at its junction with the B4405 to Bryncrug. There is a bus stop here for Nos 2 (Aberystwyth – Dolgellau – Caernarfon) and 30 (from Tywyn).

Minffordd Hotel (0654 761665)

This old drovers' inn dates back to the late 17th century. Michael Faraday, who discovered electricity, is just one of the celebrities who have found hospitality here in the past. Its location is superb. Unfortunately, it is no longer a true pub. It is a seasonal hotel, open from March to November. On weekday evenings, from 7.30pm, it is possible to book a meal with which drinks may be served. The price of a meal was £17 in 1993. The chef relishes vegetarian challenges. Residents (it's dinner, bed and breakfast only) may also enjoy a meal with drinks on Sunday evenings. You are advised to book this special occasion well in advance.

Cadair Idris

Cadair Idris is a mountain that demands that you take the challenge of going straight for its 2928 feet high summit. It is the male counterpart to the slightly higher female shyness of Aran Fawddwy. 'The Chair of Idris' is apparent for miles around. Idris was a giant, a philosopher and an astronomer. He was also a poet and 'tis said that if you spend a night at the summit of Cadair Idris you too will become a poet, or suffer death or madness in the attempt. Expect to suffer mist and bad weather at the top, even on a fine day down at Minffordd. Come suitably attired, wear good boots and carry some food and drink. The round trip could take you five hours, so allow plenty of time to descend in daylight.

The woodland at the start of this walk is a National Nature Reserve, so please keep to the path. Most of Snowdonia used to be covered by sessile oak forest such as this. The extensive repairs to the path, complete with many steps, are a necessary and well-executed response to the demands of walkers' feet. Many think (wrongly) that Cadair Idris is second only to Snowdon as the highest mountain in Wales (it isn't even the highest mountain in Meirionnydd). It may well be the second most popular mountain with walkers, however. This has been the case for a couple of centuries now. A little old lady once even sold drinks at the hut on the summit. As Charles Darwin noted, 'Cadair is a grand fellow'.

Cadair Idris

The Walk

1. Go right and fork right with the B4405. Turn right into the car park, take the kissing-gate at its end and go right along the track. Bear left with a gravel path, take another kissing-gate and follow a waymarked track. Turn right through a gate into the sessile oak woodland.

2. Keep to the path through the wood. In many ways, these steps are the toughest part of the climb, so take heart, it will become easier!

3. Go through a small gate to follow the path on the open mountainside. There is a short cut which climbs steeply ahead but the less experienced are warned to follow the main path, keeping above the stream on your right. This climbs gently into Cwm Cau. Bear left, unless you wish to divert to the waters of Llyn Cau, the lake in the dramatic amphitheatre ahead.

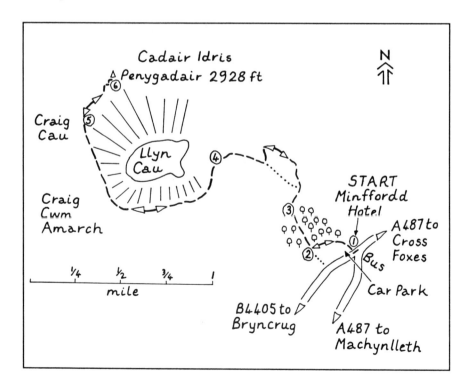

4. Having forked left, follow the path as it climbs steeply. Small cairns now act as waymarks, both to help you find your way in the mist and to encourage you not to spread the erosion. A vantage point allows a fine view of Llyn Cau, down on your right. This is a classic corrie or cirque (if you can remember your geography lessons about glaciation). Keep to the cairned path which winds steeply upwards. Reach the top of Craig Cau (this preceding peak plus the fact that the start is close to sea level means that you will actually climb well over 3000 feet on this walk.

5. Bear slightly left, away from the cliff, to descend safely from Craig Cau. Contemplate the 'chute' down to the lake on your right. Your author always associated it with a party of dentists with whom he took this short-cut once. The final ascent involves short steep zigzags to the summit cairn.

6. Retrace your steps with care back down to Minffordd. Mist can descend quickly, so it is an advantage to return by the way you ascended if the weather does turn for the worse. On a fine day, it's a delight to relax and enjoy the views in the other direction.

25. MALLWYD

Route: Brigands' Inn, Mallwyd – Bron-camlan – Dyfi Forest – Foel Dinas – Buckley Pines Hotel – Cwm-Cewydd – Brigands' Inn, Mallwyd

Distance: 9 miles

Map: O.S. Outdoor Leisure 23 (Snowdonia – Cadair Idris area)

Start: The Brigands' Inn, Mallwyd (Grid reference: SH 863125)

Access: Mallwyd is at the junction of the A458 from Welshpool and the A470 (from Cardiff to Llandudno Junction). Buses run here on certain days, currently from Machynlleth (the nearest British Rail station) on Wednesdays and Saturdays and from Dolgellau on Tuesdays and Fridays all year round plus Thursdays in the summer. Take bus No. S18 from Machynlleth and No. 27 from Dolgellau. Mallwyd is at the very edge of the public transport network, but isn't this good reason to rise to the challenge? Telephone 0286 679378 for the latest timetable information.

The Brigands' Inn, Mallwyd (0650 531208)

This is where George Borrow 'entered the Inn and seeing a comely looking damsel at the bar' asked for supper and a bed, according to his 'Wild Wales' (1862). She conducted him 'into a neat sanded parlour where a good fire was blazing'. You can spend the night here too, as the actress Vanessa Redgrave did a few years ago. It's not recorded if she stayed in room seven, but that's where the ghost of a lady has often been reported. The food is first-class, while the opening hours are 11 am to 11 pm on weekdays (12 noon to 3 pm and 7 pm to 10.30 pm on Sundays). This is the authentic Brigands' Inn which used to display weapons used by the notorious Red Bandits of Mawddwy ('Gwylliaid Cochion Mawddwy'), although it is named the Peniarth Arms on the 1902 Ordnance Survey map. The Inn dates from at least 1488, well before the brigands were exterminated. An experienced guide (yours truly) is available for a modest daily fee.

The Buckley Pines Hotel, Dinas Mawddwy (0650 531261)

Stop here for some real ale. There's food and accommodation too (plus the experienced local guide). The opening hours are 11 am to 11 pm on weekdays (12 noon to 3 pm and 7 pm to 10.30 pm on Sundays). Originally the Buckley Arms, this hotel was erected shortly after the opening of the Mawddwy Railway in 1868, when Edmund Buckley, who had acquired the Manor in 1856, was elevated to the baronetcy. It was mostly built in the then revolutionary material of reinforced concrete.

The Dolbrodmaeth Inn, Dinas Mawddwy (0650 531333)

New owners have overcome adversity to re-open this favourite inn just across the Afon Dyfi from the Meirion Mill (passed on this walk between the Buckley Pines Hotel and the Brigands' Inn), just as this book was going to press. Once the home of the slate quarry's agent, the building was burnt down in 1982. It has recently been rebuilt to present-day energy conscious standards with the personal attention of the owners. Real ale is served, while there is food available even late at night. Vegans and vegetarians are most welcome. Bed and breakfast accommodation is available, while campers can pitch their tents in the tranquil grounds. Opening hours are 11am to 11pm on weekdays, noon to 3pm and 7pm to 10.30pm on Sundays.

Mallwyd

Travellers have passed this way for thousands of years, at least since the Romans adopted the road which follows a similar route to the modern A458 and linked Wroxeter with Sarn Helen at Brithdir. For a period of centuries until 1555, what was then a remote, thickly-wooded valley was a place travellers came to at their peril. The Red Bandits established an independent enclave, sustained by brigandage.

Their end is recorded as happening in two stages during the tough Tudor rule of Queen Mary. Eighty of the red-haired brigands were caught on Christmas Eve, 1554, at nearby Collfryn (Hill of Loss). Baron

Lewis Owen executed them, including little Jac Goch, whose mother exposed her breasts and vowed that they had given suck to others who would wreak vengeance. They did, on the significant date of Hallowe'en (the ancient Celtic New Year's Eve), 1555. The Baron was ambushed near Mallwyd and killed by at least 30 arrows. This prompted a final round-up of the surviving brigands.

But what were there origins? Theories abound, with a band of Irish outlaws coming over in 1114 to help Owain, Prince of Powys and son of Cadwgan, son of Bleddyn, in his fight with King Henry I of England over the beautiful Nest, the favourite. It is a fact, however, that the only reference to Mawddwy in the Mabinogion (ancient Welsh literature) refers to a Cynwrig Frygoch (meaning red-freckled). Coming from the story about 'The Dream of Rhonabwy', this suggests that Red Bandits could have been here in the time of King Arthur, in the sixth century.

King Arthur was here in the sixth century, in fact he fought his last battle here at Camlan. There is a booklet about this, entitled 'Arthur's Camlan', available locally, including at the Brigands' Inn, Mallwyd. His nephew, St. Tydecho (whose mother was Anna of Gwent, King Arthur's sister), built the church at Mallwyd, which was already an ancient holy spot. The original altar may be incorporated in the external wall behind the present altar which is, unusually, at the northern end of the church.

St. Tydecho gained for this valley the right of sanctuary for 'one hundred ages' (as recorded in a medieval document whose photocopy and translation can be seen further up the valley in Llanymawddwy Church, where St. Tydecho's bones lie under the altar). There is good reason to add about 35 years to the date 520 carved over the inner entrance to Mallwyd Church. The Celtic Church may have dated its years from Jesus' baptism by John (or, even, from the crucifixion). The 'one hundred ages' of sanctuary could have started in 555. The human body seems to 'age' every ten years, making the right of sanctuary effective for a total of 1000 years, which brings us to 1555, when the brigands were wiped out.

Mallwyd Church has a porch dating from 1641. Curious bones adorn it. These were ploughed up in a nearby field. They could be a reminder that this valley was once flooded. Minllyn, where the Buckley Pines Hotel stands, means 'by the edge of the lake' and must have acquired this name in historical times. Perhaps King Arthur's sword was cast into the lake here after the Battle of Camlan.

Dr. John Davies was the rector here from 1604 to his death in 1644. A graduate of Jesus College, Oxford, he received his doctorate in 1616. He married a sister of Dr. Richard Parry, the Bishop of Asaph under whose name the revised edition of the 1588 Welsh Bible was published. This revision was mostly the work of Dr. John Davies, however. He also worked on a Grammar, published in 1621, and a Welsh/Latin Dictionary, published in 1632. Dr. Davies, who lies buried in Mallwyd Church, was also responsible for the erection of the Pack Horse Bridge over the River Dyfi, presumably where the Roman road forded the river, just after this route passes the Buckley Pines Hotel.

The tradition for the Battle of Camlan taking place here was recorded by a local bard, Thomas Davies (bardic name, Tegwyn), whose book 'Dinas Mawddwy a'i Hamgylchoedd' won an Eisteddfod prize in 1893. There is plenty of place name evidence, with this route climbing Bryn Cleifion (meaning 'the hillside of the bruised or wounded') to overlook Camlan before following the Roman road east towards Nant-y-Saeson, where the traitor Modred's Saxon allies camped the night before the battle. Bones and weapons were unearthed when the station (now a coffee shop within the grounds of the Meirion Mill) and the Buckley Pines Hotel were built. There must have been a fort (or 'dinas') at this strategic spot and it may be what seems to be earthworks in the field behind the old station.

The Walk

(A shallow stream has to be forded twice on this walk)

1. With your back to the Brigands'Inn, go ahead (with care!) across the A470 and turn right along the verge to the roundabout. Turn left to follow the minor road which eventually crosses a bridge over the River Dyfi to join another minor road. Turn left up this and pass Bryn Ffynnon and a signposted path going through a gate on your right. Look out for a second signposted path on your right.

2. Turn sharply right to take a gate and follow the second signposted

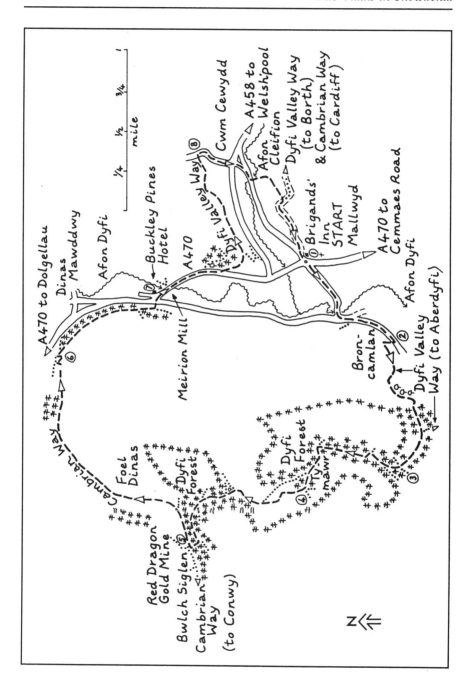

path. This climbs along the access track to Bron-camlan. Turn left with it just before the house to keep climbing gradually with the track. There is a fence on your right at first, then you cross open pasture and bear right down to where a stream goes under the track. Continue through a gate and uphill overlooking a steep tree-clad slope on your left. Fork right uphill towards the edge of the Dyfi Forest, with its conifer trees. Don't take the gate ahead at what is your last view down the Dyfi Valley. Instead, turn right to walk with the forest on your left. Turn left when you reach a stile in its perimeter fence and follow a path between plantations of conifer trees. Come to a forest track which has crossed a cattle grid on your left. Leave the Dyfi Valley Way here by turning right and following the track downhill.

3. Go ahead across another firm forest track at a junction and turn half-right downhill. Maintain this direction when another forest track comes in to join yours from your left. Climb with views of a valley on your left through the trees. Pass a waymarked path going sharply right uphill. Follow the track around a bend on your left. Pass Ty Mawr and bear right to take the higher of two gates ahead. Walk with the forest on your right and a fence and view across the valley on your left. Bear left when you come to a waymark post and follow the descending path which begins beside the fence on your left. Continue between trees to reach a stile in the bottom fence ahead. Cross this and go ahead by fording the stream (Nant Blaen-y-cwm). Climb to a signpost beside a track.

4. Turn right along the track. Walk with a fence on your left and above the stream on your right. Go ahead to ford the stream again and pass Cae abatty on your right. The name of this field indicates that it once belonged to an abbey – probably the Cistercian abbey of the Blessed Virgin Mary which used to stand near Welshpool, Powys. Perhaps the dissolute monks came here to repent – the first abbot eloped with a nun. Continue over a flat bridge across the stream. Pass a ruined farm building (Cae abbatty's) and cross a stile in the fence ahead to follow the path into the forest. Pass between more ruined buildings (Blaen-y-cwm) and climb with the track to a fork. Bear left and uphill between the trees. Reach a waymarked fork and keep left. Climb past another ruin on your left to eventually reach a signpost beside a forest track. Go left for 10 yards then bear right up a signposted path

which climbs through the forest. Reach a waymarked path junction and turn right to emerge over a stile in the perimeter fence on Bwlch Siglen (the boggy pass).

5. Turn right to follow part of Tony Drake's Cambrian Way at a point some 186 miles from its start at Cardiff and with 88 miles to go to its finish in Conwy. Look out for weary backpackers! Keep the forest on your right and the impressive view down the valley towards Aran Fawddwy on the horizon on your left. Bear left away from the forest to walk with an old, broken, fence on your right along the side of Foel Dinas at a constant height of about 1000 ft. Cross a ladder stile in the fence ahead and maintain your height and direction. Admire the waterfall down the crags of Maesglase across the valley on your left. Eventually walk past a plantation of conifer trees on your left to a stile in the corner ahead. Follow the Cambrian Way as it bears left downhill along a narrow, steep, path which finally zigzags to reach a wide, firm, forest track.

The waterfall down the crags of Maesglase

6. Turn right to descend gradually with this forest track, passing above the village of Dinas Mawddwy on your left. Ignore a cross track and go ahead to descend gradually to a T junction where you do turn left to pass a garage with a useful shop on your left. Pass the war memorial, cross the A470 carefully and turn right down the pavement to the Buckley Pines Hotel on your left.

7. Continue past the Buckley Pines Hotel on your left, across the bridge over the River Dyfi ahead (but stop to notice the 17th century Pack Horse Bridge on your right) and follow the verge of the A470 until a flight of steps on your left. Turn left up the steps to cross the stile beside a signpost and bear right up to a stile in the descending fence. Continue to climb gradually and step over the new stile in the top fence. Go ahead to a stile in the fence ahead and go down to join a track (which is the old Roman road). Turn left along this, walking with a fence and a fine view over the Cleifion Valley on your right. Continue as waymarked over a boggy patch with trees and emerge over a stile into a field with a hedge on your left. Turn left over a ladder stile and turn right immediately to follow the track past the farmhouse of Pen-y-graig and down to a minor road, at a signpost.

8. Turn right to follow the road to a junction with a similar minor road at Cwm-Cewydd. Go left and soon turn right down to the A458. Cross this main road carefully and turn right to go over a bridge across the River Cleifion. Turn left immediately after the bridge to cross a stile and follow the path through an attractive patch of oak woodland above the river on your left. Go right over a field to climb through more woodland and across another field to a track. Turn right along this track. Take a gate ahead and turn right down an unclassified county road which leads you back to Mallwyd. Go left to return to the Brigands' Inn.

26. BRYNCRUG

Route: Peniarth Arms, Bryncrug – Afon Fathew – Afon Dysynni – Broad Water – Tywyn – Talyllyn Railway – Peniarth Arms, Bryncrug.

Distance: 8 miles

Map: O.S. Outdoor Leisure 23 (Snowdonia – Cadair Idris area)

Start: The Peniarth Arms, Bryncrug (SH 608034)

Access: Bryncrug is at the junction of the A493 with the B4405 two miles north east of Tywyn, where there is a British Rail station on the famous Cambrian Coast Line (Machynlleth – Pwllheli). Even closer is a station at Rhyd-yr-onen on the Talyllyn Railway, less than one mile south of Bryncrug. A ride on this narrow gauge line can be enjoyed between Tywyn and Nant Gwernol. If you want to be deposited right outside the pub at the start of this walk, however, take the No. 28 bus between Tywyn and Dolgellau. The No. 30 bus between Tywyn and Dolgellau (via Talyllyn) and the No. 59 bus between Tywyn and Machynlleth (via Corris) both stop at the bus shelter on the minor road on the other side of the village, near the church and chapels. There is a car park near this bus shelter.

The Peniarth Arms, Bryncrug (0654 711505)

Real ale is served at this pub, which dates from 1901. The great Welsh rugby star Gareth Edwards has eaten a meal here, so why not do likewise? The name refers to Plas Peniarth in nearby Llanegryn. This was the home of William Watkin Edward Wynne, the founder of the Cambrian Archaeological Association. He made Peniarth a centre of Welsh culture and opened the doors of his library, which he stocked with priceless old Welsh books and manuscripts, to scholars. The bulk of his collection is now in the National Library of Wales, Aberystwyth. The pub's opening hours are 12 noon to 3 pm and 6 pm to 11 pm Sundays to Fridays, 12 noon to 11 pm on Saturdays.

Dysynni Land

The Dysynni Valley is one of the gems of Snowdonia National Park. Here the reeds and grasses are light and delicate as the river flows into Broad Water. The estuary now has only a narrow outlet to the sea north of Tywyn, yet much of this route was a coastal inlet as recently as the 13th century.

The landscape is a variety of greens in summer but there is usually snow on the surrounding mountains in winter. This seems to glow with the reflected light of the evening sun.

Dreams come easily in a place like this, especially as you follow the embankment path beside the river. Navigation is simple and the way is flat, so it is left to the herons or other birds to jolt you back to this world. This is the most enjoyable of leisurely strolls at the foot of the moun-tains. Bird watchers will love Broad Water (there doesn't seem to be a Welsh name). Merganser, shelduck, large gull, roost, mallard, wigeon (in winter), dunlin, redshank and oyster catcher can all be seen here, as can cormorants flying overhead between the sea and their nests on Bird Rock (Craig yr Aderyn). A different kind of bird used to fill the skies here during the second world war. As you turn towards Tywyn you cross the old airfield. This was used by No. 70 (Training) Group, Farnborough. The personnel consisted of approximately 430 RAF, 100 WAAF and No 4 RAF Regiment A.A. with Bofors guns. Hurricane, Vengeance and Mantmet aircraft were based here. They were presumably engaged in target towing duties for artillery practice. St. Cadfan's Church, Tywyn, should be visited. A 'clas' or monastery was founded here in 516 by St Cadfan when he arrived from Brittany with a host of companions to renew the Christian faith in the land of their forbears.

Cadfan was the son of Eneas Lydewig and his wife Gwen Teirbron, the daughter of Emyr Llydaw (who was, possibly, the famous Emrys Wledig – Ambrosius Aurelianus, who led the Britons against the Saxons and the traitor Vortigern in the generation before King Arthur). Cadfan's cousin was Tydecho, whose church is near the start of the Mallwyd walk. Cadfan's mother was recorded as having three breasts, which would suggest shamanic powers. Cadfan went on to become the first Abbot of Bardsey Island, the holy isle of the saints. Yet he was a patron saint of warriors. Did this relation of Arthur fight as a soldier in Brittany? Was he one of the knights of the round table?

St Cadfan's church, Tywyn

Adding approximately 35 years to the Celtic Church's dates (as explained in the notes on the Mallwyd walk) would allow Cadfan to survive into the seventh century. This could fit in with the inscription in the very earliest example of Welsh on a stone kept inside the church. Dated to the early seventh century, this translates as 'the body of Cyngen is on the side between where the marks will be', then 'beneath a similar mound is extended Cadfan, sad that it should enclose the praise of the earth. May he rest without blemish'. Cyngen was the local chieftain and the 'marks' presumably refer to four standing stones in the churchyard. Not far away, behind the Natwest Bank, is St. Cadfan's holy well. This was renowned in the 18th century for curing arthritis and rheumatism. A natural chalybeate spring, it was enclosed in 1850 and baths and dressing-rooms built. The complex was closed down in the mid 1890s as it wasn't paying. It was turned into a coach house and stables.

Leaving the church and well, notice College Green. Monks attached to the .church had a college here in the 16th century. Pilgrimages were made to here and an old pilgrim's cross, the 'croes-faen' is passed on the outskirts of Tywyn. The little steam trains of the Talyllyn Railway that may pass you as you walk back towards Bryncrug, stir memories of the Rev. W. Awdry's railway books. Look out for Skarloey! The Talyllyn Railway has a gauge of 2ft 3ins and runs for 7 $1/4$ miles from Tywyn to Nant Gwernol. It was built to bring slate from the quarries· above Abergynolwyn to the main line at Tywyn. Freight trains ran along it from 1866 to 1947, when the last quarry closed. Passengers were carried from 1867 and a vigorous campaign by enthusiasts saved the line to maintain seasonal passenger services. Telephone 0654 710472 for timetable information.

Look - and listen - out for steam trains on the Talyllyn Railway

When you reach the bus shelter in Bryncrug, divert right to Capel Bethlehem to see the grave of Mary Jones. Her story is told in another walk (Mary Jones' Cottage) but she married Thomas Lewis, a weaver from Bryncrug, settled here and attended this Calvinistic Methodist Chapel.

The Walk

1. Go left from the pub to the T junction at the heart of Bryncrug. Look for the footbridge (beyond the road bridge) across the Afon Fathew and turn right over it. Cross the A493 carefully to take a kissing gate on your right and follow the signposted footpath. This goes downstream beside the river on your right.

2. Follow the embankment path as it turns left when the Afon Fathew meets the Afon Dysynni. Continue past a waymarked path going left back towards the village. Walk with the wide river on your right and go ahead over two stiles beside gates. Cross a third stile to keep with the embankment path as it approaches Broad Water. Turn left with the embankment to pass Broad Water on your right. Reach a signpost and bear left away from the water across rough but flat land to a footbridge over a drainage ditch. This is marked by an old flag pole.

3. Cross the footbridge and turn left to walk with the drainage ditch on your left. This path leads to a footbridge ahead. Cross it and turn right along a track which leads to Tywyn. Enter the town along Gwalia Road between the cinema and St. Cadfan's Church.

4. Turn left out of town along the pavement of the A493 past Holgates' Honey Factory on your right and Pall Mall Farm Caravan and Camping Site on your left. The stone pilgrims' cross ('croes-faen') is set in trees at the corner of the lane on your right. Take this lane to walk to the access track to Hen-dy, which is signposted as a right of way. Turn left up the track, continue past Hen-dy on your left but turn left through farmyard gates to reach a footbridge over the Talyllyn Railway.

5. Bear left to walk parallel to the narrow gauge railway on your left. Continue past Fach Goch Halt to reach a bridge carrying a track across the line. Do not go left over this bridge. Go ahead to keep beside the railway on your left. When you emerge at a lane, where a public footpath signpost points in the direction from which you have just come, go left along it to cross the railway by a bridge. Pass Rhydyronen Station on your left.

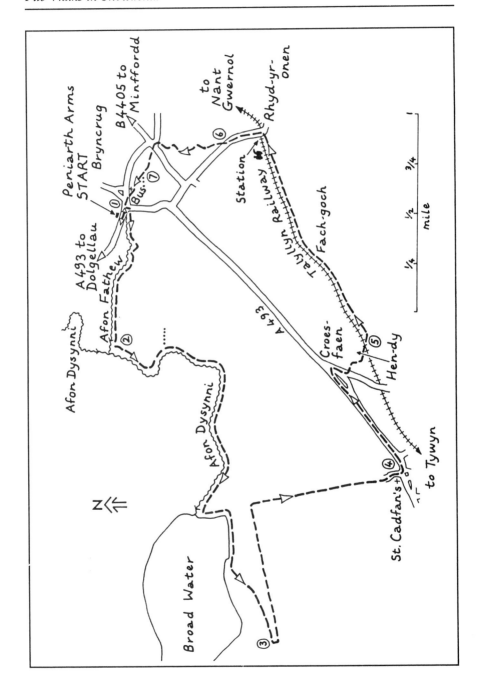

6. Come to a public footpath ('llwybr cyhoeddus') signpost on your
   right. Turn right over a slate stile in the wall and go ahead over a
   waymarked footbridge. Go left beside the stream to another signpost
   and follow the path ahead around a patch of woodland and along the
   edge of a field to a stile beside a signpost. Cross into the next field
   and turn right to walk with the hedge on your right around the edge
   of this field to a stile which leads to a narrow path from which you
   emerge across a stile beside a signpost onto a lane. Go left to a road
   which you cross to take the signposted path opposite. This leads to a
   bridge over a stream. Go ahead past a house on your left and veer
   right to a footbridge over the Afon Fathew.

7. Having crossed the bridge, turn left to reach a stile in the hedge
   ahead and continue under the wall of a chapel and its graveyard on
   your right to go over a stile beside a gate and a signpost near the bus
   shelter and a car park in Bryncrug. Divert right to visit the grave of
   Mary Jones in the graveyard of Capel Bethlehem. Go left back to the
   T junction in the heart of the village and retrace your steps to the
   Peniarth Arms, on your right.

27. ABERDYFI

Route: Britannia Inn, Aberdyfi – Golf Course – Cwm Safn-ast – Dyffryn-glyn-cul – Gwddgwion – Erw-Gwenllian – Britannia Inn, Aberdyfi.

Distance: 6¹/₂ miles

Map: O.S. Outdoor Leisure 23 (Snowdonia – Cadair Idris area)

Start: The Britannia Inn, Aberdyfi (Grid Reference SN 615960)

Access: Aberdyfi has a station on British Rail's scenic Cambrian Coast Line between Machynlleth and Pwllheli. Bus No. 29 from Tywyn or Machynlleth stops nearer the Britannia Inn, which is close to the harbour. Sea View Terrace forms part of the A493. There is a large car park near the beach, on the way to the railway bridge. There are plans to run a hovercraft service to Aberdyfi from Aberystwyth via Borth.

The Britannia Inn, Aberdyfi (0654 767426)

Ian Woosnam, the golfer, frequents this old pub, as does John Thaw of 'The Sweeney' and 'Inspector Morse'. Miners and fishermen used to comprise its clientele. Draught Bass is served, while food is available. The opening hours are 11 am to 3 pm and 6 pm to 11 pm on weekdays, 12 noon to 3 pm and 7 pm to 10.30 pm on Sundays.

Aberdyfi

Aberdyfi is an old-fashioned seaside resort, relying on sand and boats to attract holiday makers. Golfers will find a good course here between the sand dunes and the railway. Romantic tourists will climb the hill above the village to watch the sun set over Cardigan Bay and to listen for the sound of bells.

> *'Listen to the joyous bells,*
> *While through the meadow straying,*
> *O'er the hills their music swells,*
> *And this is what they're saying:*

Pretty maidens, come again..
Join us in a merry strain,
To all who live on land or main,
Say the bells of Aberdovey,
One, two, three, four, five, six,
Join us in a merry strain,
Say the bells of Aberdovey.'

So sang the comic Welsh character in Charles Dibden's late 18th century Drury land hit 'Liberty Hall'. The bells now lie under the sea, for they belong to churches in the legendary 'Cantre'r Gwaelod'. This fertile lowland in Cardigan Bay was flooded in the sixth century, if you rely on traditional accounts of Seithennin the drunkard, who neglected the sea wall. If you can believe scientists, the flooding occurred about 4000 years earlier. This could be an example of how Welsh legends have descended from Stone Age times.

Aberdyfi Golf Course, between the sand dunes and the railway

More recently, in the 18th and 19th centuries, Aberdyfi was a lead and copper mining centre. The port was important for shipbuilding as well as for fishing and trade. When the railway reached here in 1867 from Machynlleth (the line from Tywyn arrived earlier, in 1863), it opened the prospect of Aberdyfi becoming a ferry port for Ireland. There was a service to Waterford for a while. Tourism was to be Aberdyfi's industry, however, with many fine walks on its doorstep. The Victorians anglic-ised Cwm Maethlon into 'Happy Valley'. Locals camped out in the summer in order to let their houses to visitors. The golf course is on disputed ground. It was enclosed by a property developer in 1900, despite being common land. The whole village turned out to pull down fences, inspired by the Pennal Brass Band, which had come for the occasion on the train from Machynlleth. The developer gave up, but in 1927 the land was being used by Aberdyfi Golf Club. When they introduced golf on Sundays, local preachers incited crowds to assemble and prevent the Sabbath from being desecrated. Perpetual injunctions had to be made against 16 prominent opponents before the golfers could tee-off in peace on a Sunday.

The village can boast a Maritime Museum near the Outward Bound Centre. Aberdyfi's Seafront Garden Project won the Prince of Wales Award for Environmental Improvement in 1972. The Dyfi Valley Way long distance path starts its 108 mile journey to Borth via Aran Fawddwy from here. A Cambrian Coast Way linking stations on British Rail's line to Pwllheli is planned to link with the Dyfi Valley Way at Aberdyfi.

The Walk

1. Go right along the pavement of the A493 (Sea View Terrace, becom-ing Glandyfi Terrace, then Bodfor Terrace). Pass the Snowdonia National Park Visitor Centre, the harbour and the car park on your left. Continue under a railway bridge (using the route for pedestrians) and pass the access road to the British Rail Station on your left. Go ahead until, just after a letterbox on your left, a path goes left over the railway to the golf course.

2. Turn left through a gate, cross the railway carefully and go ahead through another gate. The recently diverted right of way now goes

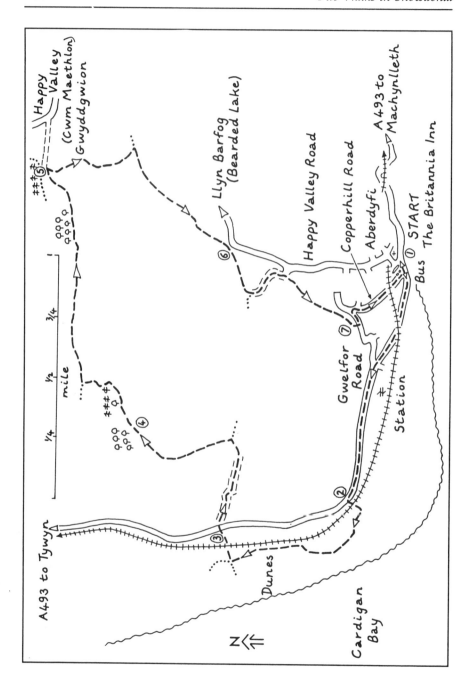

ahead and turns right for 400 yards. It then bears right back to the railway where there is a stile in the fence. Don't cross this stile! Turn left to walk with the fence and the railway on your right. Veer very slightly left to a path junction and turn right to a gate. Cross the railway carefully again and go ahead to the A493 below the cemetery.

3. Cross the A493 with care. Take the signposted right of way ahead. This is a metalled lane which passes the cemetery on your left and goes up Cwm Safn-ast. Bear left at its end to turn left through the second gate in the fence on your left. Cross a windswept moorland where an old gate post serves as a waymark. Bear right to a gate.

4. Go through the gate to take the path which descends to a gate in a lower fence. Follow it through this and down one more field to take a gate in the bottom right hand corner. Pass a pond on your right and turn right along an unclassified county road coming from Dyffryn-glyn-cûl on your left. This road is a fenced track which leads to a track junction where there are three signposts.

5. Turn sharply right along the signposted track 'to Panorama Walk and Aberdovey'. This goes through the farmyard at Gwyddgwion. Reach a stile before a stream. Cross both, bear left to a path junction and turn right to climb uphill. Go through a gate at the top and continue along a track which leads to the corner of the minor road for Llyn Barfog (Bearded Lake).

6. Turn right along a rough track. Pass a reservoir on your left and reach a signpost. Turn left to follow the track which becomes a metalled lane. Do not turn left with this lane through a gate and a short distance to join the road, however. Instead, follow the muddy path ahead. This reaches a stile and a signpost in the fence on your left after half a mile.

7. Turn left over the signposted stile. If you need to dash for a train, go right down Gwelfor Road. Otherwise, go left and turn right down Copperhill Road back to Aberdyfi's harbour and the Britannia Inn.

The Britannia Inn, Aberdyfi

We publish a wide range of titles, including general interest publications, guides to individual towns, and books for outdoor activities centred on walking and cycling in the great outdoors throughout England and Wales. This is a recent selection:

General interest:

THE INCREDIBLY BIASED BEER GUIDE – Ruth Herman
This is the most comprehensive guide to Britain's smaller breweries and the pubs where you can sample their products. Produced with the collaboration of the Small Independent Brewers' Association and including a half-price subscription to The Beer Lovers' Club. *£6.95*

DIAL 999 – EMERGENCY SERVICES IN ACTION – John Creighton
Re-live the excitement as fire engines rush to disasters. See dramatic rescues on land and sea. Read how the professionals keep a clear head and swing into action. *£9.95*

THE ALABAMA AFFAIR – David Hollett
This is an account of Britain's rôle in the American Civil War. Read how Merseyside dockyards supplied ships for the Confederate navy, thereby supporting the slave trade. The *Alabama* was the most famous of the 'Laird Rams', and was chased half way across the world before being sunk ignominiously. *£9.95*

PEAK DISTRICT DIARY – Roger Redfern
An evocative book, celebrating the glorious countryside of the Peak District. The book is based on Roger's popular column in *The Guardian* newspaper and is profusely illustrated with stunning photographs. *£6.95*

I REMAIN, YOUR SON JACK – J. C. Morten (edited by Sheila Morten)
A collection of almost 200 letters, as featured on BBC TV, telling the moving story of a young soldier in the First World War. Profusely illustrated with contemporary photographs. *£8.95*

FORGOTTEN DIVISIONS – John Fox
A unique account of the 1914 – 18 War, drawing on the experience of soldiers and civilians, from a Lancashire town and a Rhineland village. The book is well illustrated and contains many unique photographs. *£9.95*

ROAD SENSE – Doug Holland
A book for drivers with some experience, preparing them for an advanced driving test. The book introduces a recommended system of car control, based on that developed by the Police Driving School. Doug Holland is a highly qualified driving instructor, working with RoSPA. *£5.95*

Books of Walks:

There are many books for outdoor people in our catalogue, including:

RAMBLES IN NORTH WALES
– Roger Redfern

HERITAGE WALKS IN THE PEAK DISTRICT
– Clive Price

EAST CHESHIRE WALKS
– Graham Beech

WEST CHESHIRE WALKS
– Jen Darling

WEST PENNINE WALKS
– Mike Cresswell

STAFFORDSHIRE WALKS
– Les Lumsdon

NEWARK AND SHERWOOD RAMBLES
– Malcolm McKenzie

NORTH NOTTINGHAMSHIRE RAMBLES
– MAlcolm McKenzie

RAMBLES AROUND NOTTINGHAM & DERBY
– Keith Taylor

RAMBLES AROUND MANCHESTER
– Mike Cresswell

WESTERN LAKELAND RAMBLES
– Gordon Brown

WELSH WALKS:
Dolgellau and the Cambrian Coast
– Laurence Main and Morag Perrott

WELSH WALKS:
Aberystwyth and District
– Laurence Main and Morag Perrott

MOSTLY DOWNHILL:
Leisurely walks in the Lake District
– Alan Pears

WEST PENNINE WALKS
– Mike Cresswell

– all of the above books are currently £6.95 each

CHALLENGING WALKS IN NORTH-WEST BRITAIN
– Ron Astley *(£9.95)*

WALKING PEAKLAND TRACKWAYS
– Mike Cresswell *(£7.95)*

Long-distance walks:

For long-distance walks enthusiasts, we have several books including:

THE GREATER MANCHESTER BOUNDARY WALK
– Graham Phythian

THE THIRLMERE WAY
– Tim Cappelli

THE FURNESS TRAIL
– Tim Cappelli

THE MARCHES WAY
– Les Lumsdon

THE TWO ROSES WAY
– Peter Billington, Eric Slater,
Bill Greenwood and Clive Edwards

THE RED ROSE WALK
– Tom Schofield

FROM WHARFEDALE TO WESTMORLAND:
Historical walks through the Yorkshire Dales
– Aline Watson

THE WEST YORKSHIRE WAY
– Nicholas Parrott

– all £6.95 each

The Best Pub Walks!

Sigma publish the widest range of "Pub Walks" guides, covering just about every popular walking destination in England and Wales. Each book includes 25 – 30 interesting walks and varied suitable for individuals or family groups. *The walks are based on "Real Ale" inns of character and are all accessible by public transport.*

Areas covered include

Cheshire • Dartmoor • Exmoor • Isle of Wight • Yorkshire Dales • Peak District • Lake District • Cotswolds • Mendips • Cornwall • Lancashire • Oxfordshire • Snowdonia • Devon

… and dozens more – all £6.95 each!